An Overview of the
New Testament
for Young Christians

John *Maxted*

An Overview of the

New Testament

for Young Christians

AN OVERVIEW OF THE NEW TESTAMENT
FOR YOUNG CHRISTIANS
By: John Maxted
Copyright © 2013
MGL MULTILINGUAL
All Rights Reserved

Published by
American Printing & Publishing
5844 S. 194 ST.
Kent, WA 98032

ISBN: 9781927521373

Cover design by Danielle Elzinga

All Scripture quotations from the
King James Version unless otherwise noted.

Second Printing ~ 300 - 11 - 18

Printed in USA

Dedication

This book is dedicated to my five sons. The robes of Aaron were handed on to his sons after him. My prayer has always been that these five men, whom God has given to my beloved wife and I, will live to the glory of God.

Table of Contents

Introduction

I was a young man of twenty when I first met Tom Dear. At that tender age I had been appointed art director of Russell T. Kelly Advertising Agency and the creative chief, and my boss was Tom. He was a man of God who lived his Christianity and took every opportunity to impart Biblical truths to me. I consumed everything he told me of the Bible. I had been a devout church boy from my childhood but knew absolutely nothing of Scriptural truth. At this point in my life I was starving to understand the Bible and God graciously brought dear Tom into my life.

When I left Hamilton, Ontario to take up my position as Art Director at Crawley Films Ottawa, Tom gave me my first Bible exposition, *"Revelation of Jesus Christ"* by T. B. Baines. Imagine! From that point on my burning desire was to know the Scriptures. My library grew very quickly.

On November 11, 1951 my beloved wife and I took our place at the Lord's table in Ottawa. That was the beginning of my experiences with those called brethren.

I do not intend to say much about this group of Christians except that I do not believe that there was any other group that so studied and analysed the Bible as they did. I shall always thank my God for bringing me to this place that was a source of Scriptural truth and understanding. It was from these brethren teachers and writers that I accumulated much of what I know today.

It was not until I was around 74 that a most miraculous event took place. If ever I saw the hand of God moving in my life it was at this time.

For about 20 years we had a Filipino housekeeper called Teresita (Tita). We loved her very much and she was very faithful with us. We had never met any of her family but one day in 2002, a knock came at our front door and standing there was a handsome, silver haired gentleman who asked "Is my wife here?" I asked "Are you Tita's husband?" He was and he came into the house. The next part is a mystery to me but the hand of God was present. As the angels of God stood at Abraham's tent door this man, André Bujold was standing beside me. What was said or why it was said, I cannot recall. I only know that within a matter of minutes he found out that I wrote Christian articles but had never published them and he, without hesitating, asked if he could have them and he would look after the technical side of things, such as typing, computer work and printing. If I had advertised in a newspaper for a man to do this job, I could not have found anyone more qualified than he, who was to become my beloved friend, that the Lord had sent to see that my feeble efforts written over 60 years would be published.

One of my basic desires as a young man was to set down a simple outline of the books of the Bible. I wish there had been a similar work available to me as a young Christian. I have sought in each of the books of the New Testament to give the theme, the common words used, and the thrust of the teaching. My hope is that a young person can pick it up and use it as a spring board to each book.

You will notice that some of the expositions are very short and some are long. It is my practice to pray exceedingly before writing so that I will have the mind of the Spirit of God in all that I put down and not mislead in any way.

I have sought to be as simple and understandable as I can, so that it does not become ponderous nor heavy for my young reader.

It is for you, my dear young brother and sister, that I have expended a great deal of time and effort in my elder years to seek to impart to you these precious truths that the Spirit of God has been pleased to open to me. It brings great joy to my heart when I meet a young Christian who is digging into the Word of God. There is no richer way that we can spend our time. God has been pleased to open His mind and heart to us and *"made known unto us the mystery of His will"* (Eph. 1:9).

Remember *"The secret things belong unto the Lord our God: but those things which are revealed belong unto us and to our children for ever"* (Deut. 29:29). May God bless each one of you who seek to grow in grace and in the knowledge of our Lord and Saviour Jesus Christ. *"To Him be glory both now and forever. Amen"* (2 Pet. 3:18).

An Overview of the Gospels
Matthew, Mark, Luke & John

It is not my intention to go into the details of the four Gospels but rather to give an overview to show the similarities and contrasts between the four books.

Matthew, Mark and Luke are known as the synoptic Gospels, (synoptic- "together", optic- "seeing"; thus, "seeing together"). I leave it to others to write about the background and historicity of these books. My intent is to seek to show the themes and patterns of each book primarily for our young brothers and sisters who desire some assistance in understanding the thoughts and words contained therein.

My dear wife had a ring with 5 stones in it, each one representing one of our five sons. Each stone had many facets that made the light reflected from them different in each case. Each was different from the other, yet unity is brought about because they are held together by a golden band. Such are the four Gospels. Each has its own beauty and though they differ in describing the life of Christ, yet unity is brought about by the Spirit of God. The Spirit of God is the golden band.

Only one miracle of the many performed by Christ is recorded in the four Gospels; the feeding of the five thousand.

Matthew is the most Jewish of them all. It presents the Lord Jesus as Israel's promised Messiah. It is primarily to show the Jewish nation, from their own Scriptures, the many evidences in Jesus' life that were prophesied in their own Bible. There are more quotations from the Old Testament in Matthew than in any of the other Gospels.

The differences may be slight but they are marked. For instance we do not read of *"swaddling clothes"* in Matthew. This would not be fitting for a king.

There is the genealogy of Christ in Matthew and Luke, but not in Mark and John. Mark presents Christ as the perfect servant so it would not be fitting to have His genealogy there, nor is there one in John because we see Christ there as the eternal Son of God; the One who has no genealogy, for *"in the beginning was the Word, and the Word was with God, and the Word was God"* (John 1:1) a beginning, as it were, without a beginning.

We have the words *"Eli, Eli, lama sabachthani"* (Matt. 27:46, Mark 15:34) which Jesus uttered on the cross of Calvary only in Matthew and Mark. Why not in Luke and John? Each Gospel differs as to the words which were put over Jesus' head on the cross. Simply put them all together and you have the full statement.

We have a great deal of prophecy in Matthew; e.g. chapters 24, 25 which we do not have in John. Indeed prophecy is almost non-existent in John.

Luke is more concerned with the moral illustrations and teachings of Jesus and is not chronological. He was "the beloved physician" and used to opening bodies; but in Luke he is used to open men's souls. Indeed "opening" is characteristic of Luke. The key expression in Luke is *"What shall I (we) do?"* What question could be more used to search men's hearts and souls than this. If you came to me with a great problem and said "What should I do?" I would have to have you unlock your heart and thoughts to me before I could give you an intelligent answer. Following are the various times this question is asked: People (ch. 3:10), *"What shall we do"*, Publicans (ch. 3:12), *"What shall we do"*, soldiers (ch. 3:14), *"What shall we do"*, the man in the synagogue (ch. 4:34), *"What have I to do with thee"*, Pharisees (ch. 6:11), *"What they might do"*, certain lawyer (ch. 10:25), *"What shall I do"*, the unjust steward (ch. 16:3), *"What shall I do"*, a certain ruler (ch. 18:18), *"What shall I do"*, a certain blind man (ch. 18:41), *"What wilt thou that I shall do"*. It is most interesting and poignant that the last questioner is God the Father Himself, the Lord of the vineyard, (ch. 20:15), *"What shall I do,"* and finally (ch. 23:31), *"What shall be done in the dry,"* and (ch. 23:34), *"They know not what they do."* There are seven openings in the last chapter alone; count them. Luke, I repeat, is a book of openings.

This is important to notice. Various men's thoughts and hearts are opened up, e.g. the rich farmer, the certain young ruler, etc.

I leave the reader to find the seven openings in the last chapter of Luke. It is most important to note these two things in Luke because they give the complete tenor of the book.

Mark, as I have written, has no genealogy because the Lord Jesus is presented as the perfect servant. The key verse to the gospel, which has the fewest chapters, is chapter 10:45, *"For even the Son of Man came not to be ministered unto, but to minister and to give His life a ransom for many."* The two words that mark a servant, *"straightway"* and *"immediately"* are common in Mark as the words one gives to a servant.

It seems almost an aside in Genesis 37:15 that we read of Joseph *"wandering in the field."* Why is this incident recorded for it has nothing to do with the substance of the chapter? I believe it is to show that the anti-type always comes short of the type. It could never be said of Jesus that He was found *"wandering in the field."* He came to do His Father's will and this He did *"straightway"* and *"immediately."*

The division of Matthew is the 12th chapter where Jesus is accused of doing His divine work through the power of Beelzebub. This was blasphemy for it was a heinous sin spoken against the Holy Ghost. This is the unforgiveable sin of the nation of Israel. It is not a personal sin but the sin of a nation. Before this Jesus had commanded His apostles *"Go not into the way of the Gentiles...but go rather to the lost sheep of the house of Israel"* (Matt. 10:5-6). But because of this terrible sin against the Holy Spirit (in the 12th chapter), Jesus turns from them and goes to the Gentiles (ch. 15:21). In this chapter He meets a Gentile woman who pleads with Him to cure her daughter. Jesus refuses to speak to her at first for she was a Gentile and He has not heard the word from her lips which would unlock His grace towards her. He said *"I am not sent but unto the lost sheep of the house of Israel"* (v. 24). In spite of this she came and worshipped Him and cried, *"**Lord** help me"* (v. 25). This unlocked His heart to her, for *"whosoever shall call on the name of the Lord shall be saved"* (Acts 2:21), and *"no man* can say that Jesus is the Lord, but by the Holy Ghost" (1 Cor. 12:3). Jesus then answered her and said, *"it is not meet to take the children's bread and to cast it to dogs"* (v. 26). The Jews looked upon Gentiles as unbelieving dogs. The Gentile woman takes a very humble place. She acknowledges that she is a Gentile but yet *"dogs eat of the crumbs which fall from their masters' table"* (27). What lowliness, what humbleness. Jesus cannot refuse such faith and so He gave her her desire. *"And her daughter was made whole from that very hour"* (v. 28).

Up to chapter 12, as I have explained, Jesus and His disciples were commissioned to go only to the House of Israel. But after the Jews committed the unpardonable sin against the Holy Spirit, Jesus now turns to the Gentiles. This is why I believe we find in Matthew two men in the tombs (ch. 8:28), two blind men following Jesus (ch. 9:27) and two blind men sitting by the way side (ch. 20:30), it encompasses both Jew and Gentile. In Mark and Luke there is only one in all three cases. In John we have none of this recorded.

Matthew's gospel is dispensational in character. As has been said, it is the most Jewish. Matthew, Mark and Luke are called the synoptic Gospels. John is more universal.

The expression, *"the kingdom of heaven,"* is exclusive to Matthew. *"The kingdom of God,"* which we find in Mark and Luke is found only 4 times in Matthew. The *"kingdom of heaven"* is found exclusively in Matthew except for two times in Luke 11. Neither expression is found in John. Why is this? The kingdom of heaven is the kingdom in mystery with the King absent. It takes in apostates and those who are not real. Perhaps this is why it is so used in Matthew, because of apostate Israel and the Gentiles being often the subject. The kingdom of God, on the other hand, refers to those who are true believers. There are instances when both expressions are used e.g. Matthew 18:3. *"Except ye be converted and become as little children, ye shall not enter into the kingdom of heaven"*. In Mark 10:14 it is *"The kingdom of God"* as also in Luke 18:16. The expression *"Lord, Lord,"* as in Matthew 7:21 would be used by those who are not real. *"Not everyone that saith unto me, Lord, Lord, shall enter into the kingdom of heaven; but he that doeth the will of my Father."* We cannot be dogmatic about these two expressions, for at times they are inter-changeable. One would think that Matthew 7:21 should be *"the kingdom of God,"* but it is not so. That is why I say we cannot be dogmatic about applying these two expressions. But speaking in general terms the two definitions given are correct.

The genealogy in Matthew is found in perfect divisions of three sections of 14 verses each going back to Abraham, the father of the faithful. There are three women who prostituted themselves and one Gentile in this genealogy: Rahab (Rachab) *"the harlot"*, Bathsheba (though she is not named but said to be *"her that had been the wife of Urijah"*), Tamar who disguised herself as a prostitute and had a child *"Pharez"* by her father-in-law and Ruth the Gentile Moabite who married Boaz are in this genealogy. This is matchless grace on God's part.

In Luke the lineage is through Nathan, David's son; in Matthew through Solomon because in Matthew we get the kings of Judah.

In Matthew, I repeat, Israel's King is rejected in chapter 12. Israel as a nation had committed the unpardonable sin. Christ curses the fig tree which withers and dies (Matt. 21:19). The fig tree in type is Israel nationally, the grape vine is Israel as a bearer of fruit, the olive tree is Israel as a light bearer, and the bramble bush is Israel as worthless to God (Judg. 9:8-14).

In Matthew chapters 5, 6, and 7 we get the sermon on the mount, known as "the beatitudes." In all of these verses we do not have quotations from the Old Testament which is common in the rest of Matthew, because this gives us the character of those who shall be part of the coming kingdom (see Matt. 6:10 – future tense).

The expression, *"Son of Man,"* is found 84 times in the Gospels and not at all in the Epistles. It is only found 3 times outside of the Gospels (Acts 7:56; Heb. 2:6 and Rev. 1:13). It is found also numerous times in the book of Ezekiel where he is called *"son of man."* I do not know why this is.

Matthew chapter 16 is a very important chapter in that it is here that the church is first mentioned in the Bible. *"Thou art Peter,* (little stone) *and upon this rock* (Christ Himself) *I will build my church"* (v. 18). In Peter's 1st epistle he speaks of Christ being the *"living stone"* (1 Pet. 2:4), as the *"Chief corner stone"* (ch. 2:6), *"the head of the corner"* (ch. 2:7) and *"a stone of stumbling, and a rock of offence"* (ch. 2:8). (Also in 1 Cor. 10:4 and Deut. 32:4, 31, etc."). In chapter 2:5 Peter refers to believers as *"ye also, as lively* (quickened) *stones, are built up a spiritual house, an holy priesthood."*

In Matthew 24:32 the fig tree (Israel nationally) is again brought into blessing: *"Now learn a parable of the fig tree; when his branch is yet tender* (when Israel is again a young revived nation) *and putteth forth leaves, ye know that summer is nigh."*

In Matthew 27 the whole world is arraigned against Christ. The chief priests and elders (v. 1), Judas (v. 4), Pilate's wife seeks to turn her husband away from Jesus (v. 19), Pilate rejects Him (v. 26), all the people cried for His blood (v. 25), the soldiers mock Him (vv. 27-31), the two thieves revile Him (v. 44), God forsakes Him (v. 46) and His own disciples also forsake Him (ch. 26:56). See also Acts 4:27.

In the Gospels when Jesus speaks to the multitude by the seaside, it is to the people at large. Whereas when He speaks and explains His parables He takes His own into the house (Mark 2:1). Faith is found in the house (v. 5), the Word is preached in the house (v. 2), the Word is revealed in the house (Matt. 13:36), the house is the pillar and ground of the truth (1 Tim. 3:15), judgment begins in the house (1 Pet. 4:17, 1 Cor. 11:30), Jesus is Son over His own house (Heb. 3:6), God is in the house (Gen. 28:17, Ps. 89:7), holiness becomes His house (Ps. 93:5), it is a spiritual house (1 Pet. 2:5) and the house contains the household (Eph. 2:19).

In Mark chapter 4:32 in reference to *"the kingdom of God,"* the words used are *"so that the fowls of the air may lodge under,"* whereas in Matthew 13:32 using the same parable of the mustard seed, the words are, *"so that the birds of the air come and lodge in."* As is typical in Matthew it is the *"kingdom of heaven,"* whereas in Mark it is *"the kingdom of God."*

The mustard seed represents the beginning of Christianity. It has grown into a great tree (Matt. 13:31-32). *"The birds of the air lodge in the branches thereof."* This is evil doctrine infiltrating the church and corrupting it. Birds are sometimes used in an evil sense in the Bible (Gen. 15:11).

In Mark 10 we have three things that are pleasant in nature: marriage, children and good men. Chapter 14 is the longest chapter in Mark and is similar to Matthew 26 and John 12, except Simon the leper is not mentioned in John. Luke chapter 7 is different. In Matthew and Mark Jesus is dining in the house of Simon the leper and the ointment is poured on Jesus' **head**. In Luke it just says he was in the house of *"one of the Pharisees"* and *"a woman in the city"* anointed Jesus' **feet** with the ointment. In John's gospel a similar event is recorded but it tells us that this occurrence was in the house of Lazarus and it was his sister Mary that poured the precious ointment on the feet of Jesus. Matthew and Mark thus are the same but Luke is another case as is that which is recorded in John.

One peculiarity in Mark that one does not find in the others is the use of the Greek aorist tense. We do not have this tense in English grammar. It is the eternal present as seen by God. Ecclesiastes 3:15 gives a good explanation of this tense: *"That which has been is now; and that which is to be has already been; and God requireth that which is past."* Also with God *"one day with the Lord is as a thousand years, and a thousand years as one day"* (2 Pet. 3:8). In Mark chapter 14:32, we read *"and they came,"* using the past tense, but in verse 33 *"and He taketh."* (ch. 6:2 *"and many hearing Him,"* not *"heard Him."*) *"And they brought young children to Him"* (10:13), not "They bring young children to Him." There are many other cases. Why is this the case in Mark and not in the other Gospels?

In Luke one notices the human things in Christ's life; His birth, His childhood, etc. The Son of Man is the theme and yet as the Son of God He shines out also. (3:38, 4:41, 22:70). Luke is fond of the word *"great"* which is repeated 40 times in the gospel and 43 times in the Acts. There are always reasons behind these numerous repetitions of words or phrases one finds in the Bible.

Also in Luke we get the Son of Man's age (2:42, 3:23). Why is this? As has been said, Luke is the book of openings. In chapter 2:35, 51 we have hearts opened and in chapter 3:21 heaven opened. But in the last chapter (24) we find seven openings: opened sepulchre (v. 3); opened home (v. 29); opened Scriptures (vv. 27, 32); opened eyes (v. 31); opened hearts (v. 32); opened understanding (v. 45), and opened heavens (v. 51).

In Luke 6:13 we have the best definition of what is an apostle – a sent one; and one who is a disciple, i.e. a follower. There were only 12 apostles but there were many disciples – followers. Some of these disciples fell away and were no longer followers of Jesus. When He spoke of eating His flesh and drinking His blood in John 6:53, 56, many of His disciples left Him. *"And when it was day* (after Jesus spent the night in prayer), *He called unto Him His **disciples**: and of them He chose twelve, whom He also named **apostles**."*

The beatitudes, which take up 3 chapters in Matthew, are greatly condensed in Luke 6 where there are only 29 verses (vv. 20 to 49).

Luke 9:29 *"And as He prayed, the fashion of His countenance was altered, and His raiment was white and glistening."* While Jesus was here on earth His eternal glory was hidden but His moral glory could not be. But here, on a very rare occasion, the *shekinah* glory of the Son of God is visible. Glory is excellence on display. In John 17:5 we have Christ's eternal glory which He had with His Father *"before the world was."* But in verse 22 we have His acquired glory. *"The glory which Thou gavest me I have given them."*

In Luke 9:28 we read of the eighth day. Eight in the Bible is descriptive of a new beginning, a new order of things. What we have in Luke leads us into Paul's ministry. Luke was no doubt a Gentile doctor (Col. 4:14).

In Matthew 17:1 we are told *"after six days Jesus taketh Peter, James, and John his brother, and bringeth them up into an high mountain."* There He was transfigured before them and they saw His glory. Six is man's number. Here it is man in his responsibility Godward. In Luke 9:28 recounting the same incident, it is recorded *"and it came to pass about an eight days after these sayings".* Eight is the number for a new order. It is one number beyond seven which stands for completeness or fulfillment. Why the change in the number of days I cannot tell. Mark 9:2 has only six days.

Luke chapter 10 begins with service but ends with worship. Mary chose the better part. In chapter 12 we have waiting (v. 36), watching (v. 37) and working (v. 38).

In chapter 15 of Luke we have the well known story of the prodigal son. The prodigal impoverished his father by taking half of what his father had before his father had died. An inheritance is not in force until the death of the testator (Heb. 9:16). The only important words the son was permitted to say were, *"I have sinned"* (v. 21). The rest was redundant. The father closed his son's mouth with paternal kisses. The father gave this returning son *"the best robe"* (v. 22), the robe of righteousness (Isa. 61:10), a ring, unending love, (a ring has no ending), and shoes, that is, in type he was lifted from the earth and made a heavenly citizen.

In Matthew 25 we have another well known parable of the ten virgins. The number ten has the meaning of responsibility. Note 10,000 talents (Matt. 18:24), 10 talents (Matt. 25:28), 10 cities (Luke 19:17), 10,000 instructors (1 Cor. 4:15), a 10th of all that he had (Heb. 7:2, 4). In each case the number ten is in connection with man's responsibility.

In Luke chapter 22:9, *"They said unto Him, where wilt thou that we prepare?"* This was to be in preparation of the Passover. It was to be large, room for everyone, upper, away from the world, and furnished, nothing was needed. It was to be held at a proper, set time (v. 14). Jesus was there (v. 15) but also the traitor Judas (v. 21), and there was strife among the disciples as to which of them should be accounted the greatest (v. 24). This last characteristic has been the bane of the church down through the centuries. Jeremiah warned his servant Baruch, *"Seekest thou great things for thyself? Seek them not"* (Jer. 45:5).

The one thief's heart is opened only in Luke, the book of openings.

The Gospel According to
John
(A Closer Look)

Introduction

What can one say of the Gospel of John? The magnificence of thought goes beyond words into the spiritual realm of the divine relationship between the Son of God and His Father. God became flesh and took His place as the perfect representative of His Father, not doing His own will, even though by Him all things were and are created and by Him all things subsist or have there being (Col. 1:17). The One of whom God the Father says, *"But unto the Son He saith, 'Thy throne O God, is for ever and ever'"* (Heb. 1:8), is the same lowly Jesus on who being wearied with His journey, sat at Sychar's well and asked a village prostitute for a drink of water.

In the Gospel of John, the Son of God lays His glory by and the richness of the position that He had in eternity to become poor for our sakes (2 Cor. 8:9). He, as man, was totally dependent upon His Father. He, the creator and sustainer of all things, could say, *"I can of mine own self do nothing"* (ch. 5:30). And *"For as the Father hath life in Himself; so hath He given to the Son to have life in Himself"* (v. 26). Where could we find such statements but in the Gospel of John? God manifest in the flesh, the Word becoming flesh in perfect harmony and subject as man to the Father's will. *"Though He were a Son, yet learned He obedience by the things which He suffered"* (Heb. 5:8). The perfect man in perfect subjection to the Father's will. But we must ever keep before us that He did not cease to be what He was in eternity by whom He became in time.

This, my friend, is how I perceive my blessed Lord in John's gospel. He has won my heart for eternity and is worthy of all our worship and praise. *"Worthy of honour and of praise, worthy* by all to be adored, exhaustless streams of heavenly lays, Thou, Thou art worthy Jesus, Lord."* God had created man in His likeness and image and the first Adam failed miserably. The Creator comes, the last Adam, to bring fallen man back into His circle of love and affection. *"Then I restored that which I took not away"* (Ps. 69:4). The awesome and fearful *"I am"* of the burning bush becomes the lowly *"I am"* of John's gospel. I have not counted the numerous *"I am"* of the gospel but there are many and they are well known: *"I am the way, the truth and the life; I am the good Shepherd; I am the door; before Abraham was, I am."* Let your soul be enriched by seeking these words out. When the Pharisees questioned Jesus as to who He was, He answered them, *"Just what I have been telling you from the beginning"* (ch. 8:25, NIV).

While He was here He was the light of the world. That light shone in darkness but the darkness could not comprehend Him. He did not come to abolish the law but to fulfill it and took it out of the way and nailed it to His cross (Col. 2:14) so that you and I could go free.

The shortest biography of the Son of God is found in John 16:28: *"I came forth from the Father, and am come into the world: again, I leave the world, and go to the Father."* And again we read, *"Jesus knowing that the Father had given all things into His hands, and that He was come from God, and went to God"* (ch. 13:3). He was here in this world for the short span of 33 years, yet He turned this world upside down (Acts 17:6). They wondered at every gracious word that He uttered and yet the next moment they sought to kill Him (Luke 4:22, 28). The demons knew Him (Mark 1:34), yet those He came to seek and to save did not and sought to kill Him (John 5:18).

This then is the man Christ Jesus that we read of in John. He made the world, He came into the world, but the world knew Him not. He came unto His own and His own received Him not. *"He looked for comforters but found none"* (Ps. 69:20).

John chapter 1:14 contains one of John's favourite words: *"Beheld"* or *"behold."* *"And the Word was made flesh, and dwelt among us, (and we beheld His glory, the glory as of the only begotten of the Father,) full of grace and truth."* All through John we are given the blessed privilege of beholding Christ's glory. Please note: the word grace is found only 38 times in the Old Testament but 100 times in the New. The grace of God and the grace of our Lord Jesus Christ is not found in the Old Testament at all. The word grace is first used in the New Testament in John chapter 1:14. *"Grace and truth came by Jesus Christ"* (ch. 1:17).

The words most often used in John's gospel give us the essence of the book: *"love"*, 57 times; *"Father"*, 122 times; *"to believe"*, 100 times; *"to know"*, 54 times; and *"glory"*, 42 times.

It is not so much the multitudes that Jesus ministers to in John but individuals. In chapter 1 it is Nathaniel; in chapter 3 it is Nicodemus; in chapter 4 the woman at the well; in chapter 5 the man with an infirmity which he had for 38 years; in chapter 8 the woman taken in adultery and in chapter 9 the man born blind. In chapter 10 the Lord is presented as the Good Shepherd who is to give His life for the sheep. His grace and pardon extends to the Gentiles. *"Other sheep I have, which are not of this fold (flock): them also must I bring, and they shall hear my voice; and there shall be one fold (flock), and one Shepherd"* (v. 16). The grace of God goes over the wall to the Gentiles. *"Joseph (a type of Christ) is a fruitful bough, even a fruitful bough by a well; whose branches run over the wall"* (Gen. 49:22).

J.N.D. makes the observation that in the Gospel of John we view eternal life in Christ; in John's 1st epistle we view it in the believer. The 1st Epistle of John is an extension of the Gospel of John with the exception that much of it contains empirical statements beginning with *"we know."* In this epistle we read twice over that God is love and we also read in the first and last chapters that Jesus is intrinsically eternal life. Not that He just imparts it, but He is this in Himself. The comparison of the Son of God to the earth's sun is interesting. From our sun we receive light, energy, life and power. Its gases have been sending forth heat for eons and yet those gases are never diminished. *"In Him was life; and the life was the light of men"* (John 1:4).

What more could we say about this blessed man-God called Jesus? *"And there are also many other things which Jesus did, the which, if they should be written every one, I suppose that even the world itself could not contain the books that should be written. Amen"* (ch. 21:25). May we carry this precious book in our hearts and may God bless these feeble efforts to extol His name. Let all God's people say, Amen and Amen.

Chapters 1-11

From chapters 1 to 11 the Lord Jesus works with individual souls according to their position and need. In each case He deals differently. Sometimes He works through the heart and at others the conscience. It is beautiful and instructive to see His approach to each individual soul and to know just what He said to them in order to reach them. We can learn much from this.

Addendum: The Sanctuary In The Gospel of John

Chapter 12

THE BRAZEN ALTAR was the first object one saw when coming into the court of the people. Upon it was offered various animals for a burnt offering. (Most of Exodus). To my surprise neither the words "Brazen Altar" nor "Altar of Brass" are found in the Bible (Ex. 29:36-44). This altar was to be overlaid with brass and brass in Scripture speaks of judgment. This altar is called *"burnt offering"* (Ex. 38:1), and in type speaks of the altar of Christ going into judgment for our sins. The 12th chapter is the division of John's gospel and it begins and ends with death and resurrection (vv. 1, 24). The corn of wheat must die in order that there can be eternal fruit.

Chapter 13

THE LAVER stood just between the Altar of Brass and the veil into the holy place (Ex. 30:18). Christ leaves us an example to wash one another's feet; the body needs cleansing only once. This is done by the blood of Christ once for all. The washing of the feet is for defilement by the way. We can have no part with the Lord Jesus if there is not that continual washing of water by the Word (v. 10).

Chapter 14

THE SANCTUARY (Ex. 25:8), Where God dwells. Where His children are at home and at rest and where God can be worshipped unhindered (Ps. 84).

Chapter 15

THE CANDLESTICK (Ex. 26:35), As fruit bearers we are light standards for God. *"That they may see our good works* (in Christ) *and glorify our Father which is in heaven"* (Matt. 5:16).We can only shine for Him as we abide in Him and He in us.

Chapter 16

THE VEIL (Ex. 26:31), The Lord Jesus perpetually has perfect liberty to go into the Father's presence. Now by the rent veil, *"that is to say, His flesh"* (Heb. 10:20), we too have that same liberty, *"because I go to the Father"* (v. 16). *"For the Father Himself loveth you"* (v. 27). Why? *"Because you have loved me, and have believed that I came out from God"* (v. 27).

Chapter 17

THE HOLY OF HOLIES, The inner sanctuary, where Christ our Great High Priest is alone with God. This truly is the Lord's prayer. John 3:35. As, in type, Abraham gave all that he had to his son, (Gen. 24:36; 25:5).Even so the Father delivers all things into the hands of His Son.

What the Father has given the Son as found in John 17.

1. Power over all flesh (v. 2).
2. Men out of this world (vv. 2, 6, 9, 11, 24). How important this gift from the Father is to Christ when He emphasizes it so.
3. The Word (v. 8).

4. The divine commission (vv. 18, 23).

5. Glory (v. 22).

What the Son has given to His own:

1. Eternal life. This He has in Himself. It is not one of the Father's gifts to His Son. See 1st John 1:2 and 5:20. *"For as the Father hath life in Himself; so hath He given to the Son to have life in Himself"* (John 5:26).

2. The Word (vv. 8, 14).

3. The divine commission (v. 18).

4. The glory. This would be the acquired glory of the Lord Jesus. We have yet to enter into this (Rom. 8:17, 30).

It might be added that as Luke opens the thoughts and hearts of men, in John's gospel, Christ opens, in all its majesty and greatness, the heart of God. Jesus came to declare to man all that was in the Father's heart.

THE *Acts* OF THE APOSTLES

History teaches us that each generation needs its own encounter with God; it's a great awakening and each of us personally need it. A spiritual life is not inherited from our forebears. It is experienced through a personal encounter with God.

Anonymous

Introduction

"For David, after he had served his own generation by the will of God, fell on sleep" (Acts 13:36). As we read the history of the church we find that in each generation God raises up men and women with various gifts to nurture their fellow Christians. J.N.D., W. Kelly and other great scholars, men of high intellect, spirituality and knowledge were raised up during the 19th Century, *"men of renown"* (Num. 16:2). The truth of the Word of God never changes but society about us, the world in general and languages do. I fear that a young Christian of today has difficulty relating to the archaic language and use of words that our fathers in the faith used in their writings. In general modern day writers are very watered down from these great Bible scholars. The great advances in technology also has had a negative effect on reading books.

It is a very serious matter to attempt to write Scriptural expositions that are distributed to the Lord's people. The technical aspect which takes up 7/10th of producing a book is time consuming and wearisome but it must be done. But for my own part I spend a great deal of time in prayer asking God to guide me by His Spirit that what I write is the truth of God. *"My brethren, be not many masters* (teachers) *knowing that we shall receive the greater condemnation"* (Jas. 3:1). I really have only two great desires in publishing these expositions: one is that in all cases I might glorify God and exalt His Son and the

29

other is that the Lord's people might receive a blessing. If my wondrous Lord will grant me these two desires I will be eternally grateful.

It has been on my heart for many years to write the truths that I have read and heard over 60 years from a variety of teachers having their own individual slant on Scripture. I am thankful to my God that at 86 years he has given me a sharp mind that recalls a great deal of what I have gathered over this period of time. Much of what I understand has been garnered by my 60 years gathered to the Lord Jesus on the ground of the one body with those who are called brethren. I believe I can say that no group of believers have so researched or dug into Scripture as this group has. We have failed so miserably in keeping *"the unity of the Spirit in the bond of peace"* (Eph. 4:3) and I am ready to acknowledge this, but there are many writers today who have had their own or their families association with this failing group. Personally I will be eternally grateful to my Lord that at age 24 I was guided to a brethren assembly. *"I being in the way, the Lord led me to the house of my master's brethren"* (Gen. 24:27).

I have sought to use plain language and to be as succinct as I can be. I am afraid at times I have failed in this, e.g. (Acts, Hebrews) but I asked the Lord to guide me and enable me to put down as the Spirit led. With each of the 27 books I have sought to give the theme of each book and the words or phrases that are often repeated and which give what God is seeking to emphasize in each book.

These expositions have been written with the young Christian in mind and I pray with all my heart that they will get the good of them. I have often said to others that there is only one thing better for our souls than reading the Word of God and that is meditating on it. The clean animals named in the Scriptures are those who parted the hoof and chewed the cud. (Lev. 11:3) That is, we Christians should walk separate from this world and we should meditate upon God's Word.

I send this forth to my beloved young believers in the hope that it will instill in them the desire to search the Scriptures

(Acts 17:11). It rejoices this old man's heart when I meet one who is revelling in God's Holy Word. I pray that my present reader may be one of those.

Acts follows in the footsteps of the Gospels. It is written in essay form and does not contain doctrine as the Epistles do. It is the history of the birth of Christianity and the slow transition from Judaism to Christianity which we see throughout the entire book. William MacDonald aptly puts it, "it is the period when the N. T. church was throwing off the grave clothes of Judaism." The main character in the first part is the apostle Peter, the apostle to the Jews, but this changes to Paul in the second part, the apostle to the Gentiles.

There are too many indications that prove it was written by the beloved physician Luke, who hides himself in the history given of Paul. The most positive indications that Luke wrote the epistle are the opening words, *"The former treatise have I made, O Theophilus, of all that Jesus began both to do and to teach"*. A Grecian doctor writing to a Grecian friend. There is every indication throughout the book of Luke's intelligence and ability to describe in detail all that he heard and all that he had witnessed for himself. He modestly hides himself throughout and one can only tell when he actually is part of the action when the *"they"* turns to *"we"*(ch. 16:5, 7, 10).

The book begins with Jerusalem and ends with Rome; it begins with the synagogue and ends with the church; it begins with Peter, the apostle to the Jews and ends with Paul, the apostle to the Gentiles (Rom. 15:16); it begins with the Jews and ends with the Gentiles; it begins with the Sabbath and ends with the Lord's day or first day of the week (Sunday). It is from beginning to end the history of the transition from Judaism to Christianity. Luke's ability to record detail is shown in the many speeches we have in Acts. Peter in chapter 2:14, Stephen in chapter 7 and Paul in his address to the elders of Ephesus (ch. 20:17), before a great council and before both Festus and Agrippa (ch. 26) to name a few. It is said by many scholars that Luke's description of Paul's journey by boat to Rome is one of the most exact descriptions of a maritime journey of that period on record. I repeat, Luke was a man of great intelligence and had the ability to detail various events.

The apostle Peter is front and centre throughout the first part of Acts but after chapter 12 he is only mentioned once. Peter was given the keys to the kingdom by Christ in Matthew chapter 16:19. It is interesting that this bit of information is only found in Matthew, the book which concerns the Jews in the early part, but after chapter 12, the Gentiles. Peter's specific commission from a risen Christ was to minister to his own people the Jews, but as being given the keys to the Kingdom he introduced both Jews and Gentiles to those things concerning Christ and the church. As Paul says in chapter 28:28, *"Be it known therefore unto you* (the Jewish nation), *that the salvation of God is sent unto the Gentiles, and that they will hear it."*

The propagating of Christianity began at Jerusalem (Luke 24:47) and from there spread out into the Gentile world (ch. 13:49, 14:1). *"And the word of the Lord was published throughout the whole region"* so that the world was turned upside down by the preaching of this new so called sect (ch. 17:6).

Another interesting aspect of Acts is the name that seemed to be attached by the world to these early believers, *"the people of the way"* (ch. 9:2, 19:9, 22:4, 24:14, 22). The followers of Christ were first called Christians at Antioch (ch. 11:26). The plural of this word is only found once as here and in the singular only twice (ch. 26:28, 1 Pet. 4:16). Having given the general spine of the Acts of the Apostles we shall look at each chapter briefly to get the theme.

Chapter 1

The Lord Jesus having companied with His followers for forty days was received up into heaven from the same spot to which He will return, the Mount of Olives (Zech. 14:4). The Mount of Olives is about a Sabbath's day journey from Jerusalem (v. 12). The angels proclaimed to the sorrowing viewers that *"this same Jesus, which is taken up from you into heaven, shall so come in like manner as ye have seen Him go into heaven"* (v. 11). These words are referring to Christ's second coming,

Acts

the appearing (Rev. 19:11) and not the return of Christ for His church (1 Thess. 4:16). It is thought by many that the word "*same*" is one of Christ's titles (Heb. 1:12, 13:8).

In this chapter we read for the last time of Mary and Jesus' earthly family. Many times Jesus' family is mentioned in the Gospels. (Matt. 12:47, 13:55-56 etc.). We must rejoice in the knowledge that though there was a time that His own brothers and sisters did not believe in Him, we see them here in this chapter with Christ's disciples and apostles gathered together with one heart waiting for the fulfillment of the promise of the Father. (Ch. 1:4). A faithful man must be chosen to take the traitor Judas' place and Matthias was chosen by the Jewish custom of lots.

Chapter 2

Pentecost according to Leviticus 23, was 50 days after the offering of the sheaf of the wave offering. They were to count seven Sabbaths and one day after the last Sabbath which would make that day a Sunday (Lev. 23:15-16). I am continuously in awe at the perfection of the Bible and have said many times that only God could have written it. (1 Pet. 1:10-12, 2 Pet. 1:21)

Now when the Lord's day had come, the followers of Jesus were all assembled together and were all filled with the Holy Ghost. The cry of the new born church is heard by the multitude gathered together as each person heard in their own tongue the word of life.

From verse 14 to 36 we have the first speech in Acts, given by Peter in this case. He rehearsed with this great company the promise of Joel 2:28 which was partially fulfilled that day. Peter also speaks of Jesus and His death and resurrection. He sums up his speech by saying to the assembled throng "*Therefore let all the house of Israel know assuredly, that God hath made that same Jesus, whom ye have crucified, both Lord and Christ*" (ch. 2:36). It is of great importance to understand that during this time great multitudes were added to the church both real and unreal who later caused great troubles among the true church.

33

Chapter 3

Many pentecostal gifts were given and performed in the early history of the church. These gifts dissipated with the death of the apostles. This chapter contains one such miracle performed by Peter. There are more to follow. In the Scriptures the gospel of the grace of God was preached by Peter to the Jews first in Jerusalem.

Chapter 4

An infuriated Satan begins his deadly work among the early infant church, the sect of the Sadducees who neither believed in angels nor resurrection were incensed by the apostles teaching the people who preached through Jesus the resurrection from among the dead. At this time another five thousand were added to the church. The religious hierarchy of the day now taking note of the ascension of this new religion, as they saw it, and for fear it would encroach upon their domain and power, brought these preachers of this new faith before them to hear of this matter.

Again Peter as spokesman gives another speech. He tells this assembled throng that salvation is only through Jesus *"for there is none other name under heaven given among men, whereby we must be saved"* (v. 12). And *"they took knowledge of them, that they had been with Jesus"* (v. 13).

When they had heard Peter they commanded them not to speak at all or teach in the name of Jesus (v. 18). But when they let them go they went to their own company and told them all that had befallen them.

Verse 27 is important for it tells us that the whole world both Gentile and Jewish rulers and Gentile and Jewish people were arraigned against Christ.

This company along with Peter and others lifted up their hands to God and together exalted the Lord God. It must have been a wondrous, Spirit filled meeting for in verse 31 it tells us *"the place was shaken where they were assembled together; and they were all filled with the Holy Ghost, and they spake the Word of*

God with boldness." They were of one heart and one soul. What mighty power and grace was witnessed in this early church.

Chapter 5

The wiles of Satan worked in the hearts of Ananias and Sapphira. Sin in its slightest form was not tolerated in the early church. How much has changed since then. The disciples feared at the report of the death of Ananias and his wife. *"And by the hands of the apostles were many signs and wonders wrought among the people"* (v. 12). Multitudes were added to the church daily. The whole city of Jerusalem was moved by these acts and miracles performed by the apostles and brought their sick into the streets to be healed by them. Even the cities round about had heard of these miracles and brought their sick and those who were vexed with unclean spirits and the Bible tells us *"they were healed every one"* (v. 16).

These events were too much for the religious powers and the apostles were put into prison. But the angel of the Lord, by night, opened the prison doors and they went forth preaching the word of God. The authorities, when they had knowledge of these things again brought the apostles before the council made up of religious and secular groups and repeated their demands that they cease their preaching and teaching of Christ. But Peter replied *"we ought to obey God rather than man"* (v. 29). These authorities were so incensed by Peter's words that they sought to kill them. But the great Gamaliel, a teacher of the Jews and a doctor of the law warned this body that they should do nothing rash against these apostles for *"if it be of God, ye cannot overthrow it; lest haply ye be found even to fight against God"* (v. 39). And so they beat them and let them go.

Chapters 6 & 7

Again we are reminded of the rapid growth of this infant church. Jewish converts were literally pouring in to join this new religion. But we must keep in mind that many of them were not real and later brought much harm and division to this early church (1 John 2:19).

From verses 2 to 5 we realize that this new religion was beginning to reach out unto the Gentiles, for these deacons, chosen by the apostles to minister to the widows were all Greeks. The disciples were now freed of these duties to spend more time in prayer and ministry. How important it is that prayer precedes ministry. For there can be no power in ministry unless there is much time in prayer.

The word goes forth in great power so that even a great company of the Levitical priests were obedient to the faith (verse 7). And now, like a meteor, Stephen comes on the scene and the next large portion (from ch. 6:8 to 7:60) is taken up with this man of God and his speech to the *"synagogue of the Libertines"* which is remarkable for details.

I will not seek to write an exposition of this remarkable speech that fills the whole of chapter 7. I would ask my readers to just read it as it is.

Stephen having finished this Spirit inspired speech was rushed upon by an infuriated mob and was stoned to death. He sees Jesus in the heavens, standing on the right hand of God (ch. 7:55-56).

Chapter 8

Saul is for the first time introduced. Paul's digested biography is given in Philippians, chapter 3:5-6. Truly "the blood of the martyrs is the seed of the church" for at the death of Stephen and the persecution of the church the followers of Christ went everywhere preaching the word (v. 4) and seeing multitudes come to Christ.

The apostle Philip goes to Samaria and preaches Christ to them. From 2 Kings 17 we find who these Samaritans were. They were a rag tag element brought in to the north of Palestine to fill the place that the ten scattered tribes of Israel had occupied. They were despised by the Jews for they claimed they were descendants of Abraham and part of the Israelite economy. (John ch. 4:10, 21). When I was a young man I recall seeing an article in the National Geographic about the few remaining Samaritans. Whether there are any today dwelling in the north of Palestine I cannot say. But Philip's visit and preaching had joyous results.

Simon who lived in this city was a sorcerer and bewitched the Samaritans into believing that he possessed the power of God (vv. 9-10). Simon, for his own greedy purpose, joined these true proselytes and believed in his head what Philip preached but, as we see later, not in his heart. In other words he was an apostate. He sought in his ignorance to buy the gift of having the power of the Holy Ghost. Such blasphemy Peter admonishes with the stronger words and tells Simon *"thy heart is not right in the sight of God"*(v. 21). His later history is left untold.

And now from verse 27 to 40 we have the wonderful story of Philip and the Ethiopian eunuch. A seeking soul meets a man of God. This always results in blessing. Romans 10:14-15 says *"how shall they hear without a preacher? And how shall they preach, except they be sent?"* We may be able to believe in God through nature but in order to open our hearts to Christ we must have the Word of God in our hands or someone to speak it to us. (Rom. 10:8)

This event reminds us of the Queen of Sheba, who came to see Solomon for she had heard of his great wisdom and prosperity. What was it that moved this eunuch of great authority to travel all the way to Palestine? As he was reading the Septuagint version of the Bible, which differs in small points to the King James, (note the difference in words), the angel of the Lord, which was no doubt the second person of the Trinity, sends Philip to meet him. The Ethiopian cannot understand the passage he is reading in the Septuagint and asks Philip to explain it. *"And Philip preached unto him Jesus"* (v. 35). That blessed gospel has not changed in 2000 years. For *"there is none other name under heaven given among men, whereby we must be saved"* (Acts 4:12). The Ethiopian confesses his faith in Christ and asks to be baptized; to be identified with Christ. So that he cannot get his eyes on a man Philip was snatched away by the Spirit of the Lord and the eunuch goes on his way rejoicing. What a glorious story.

Chapter 9

And now we have the story of Saul's conversion. Each time he retells this occasion the light gets more brilliant. (Ch. 22:6, "*a great light*"; 26:13, "*a light from heaven, above the brightness of the sun*"). Saul's name is changed to Paul; Saul means destroyer, Paul means little (ch. 13:9).

Paul is struck blind for three days and the Lord sends a certain disciple named Ananias, a citizen of Damascus, to seek Saul out and takes him to his home. Once there Saul receives his sight once again. *"And straightway he preached Christ in the synagogues, that He is the Son of God"* (v. 20).

Those who heard Saul preach were querulous because they had heard how that this same man had persecuted the people of "the way". The Jews of Damascus sought to find Saul in order to kill him but his friends let him down by the wall in a basket. The great persecutor Saul, did not forget this indignity to his person, for no doubt some of that religious pride had not been completely eradicated for in his list of things that he suffered for Christ he mentions this event (2 Cor. 11:33). When Saul was come to Jerusalem from Damascus, Barnabas, who was to be his future companion took him to the apostles and introduced him to them.

It was about this time of Saul's conversion and the time he spent in Jerusalem that a short period of peace and rest was allowed the church and many were added to it.

Peter makes a journey to Lydda to minister to the saints there. He performs a miracle upon Aeneas. Many in Lydda moved by this miracle turned to the Lord (vv. 32-35).

A certain woman of Joppa named Tabitha, a much loved believer, dies. Peter travels from Lydda to Joppa and prays over the body of Tabitha and she receives life. Through this miracle many in Joppa turned to Christ.

Chapter 10

In this chapter, Cornelius, a centurion who lived in Caesarea and was a God fearing Gentile is introduced. He was told by an angel to send to Joppa for Peter. Cornelius sends two of his household servants to fetch Peter who lodged with Simon the tanner in Joppa. As they journeyed Peter went up upon the rooftop to pray and while there he went into a trance and had a remarkable vision. This vision given by God was to show Peter, who was a devout Jew and had nothing to do with Gentiles, that God had ordained that Gentiles also should receive the Holy Ghost. God had shown Peter that the gospel of the grace of God was to be preached to all men.

Peter returns with the servants to Caesarea and Cornelius' house who had called together many kinsmen and friends to hear Peter. Peter tells them of his vision and how he had understood that *"Who will have all men to be saved, and to come unto the knowledge of the truth"* (1 Tim. 2:4). Peter preaches the gospel to this Gentile company. Contrary to the Jewish companies who had first to be baptized before the Holy Ghost came upon them, this Gentile company received the gift of the Holy Ghost first and then were baptized.

Chapter 11

When the apostles and those of Judea heard this amazing event concerning the Gentiles of Caesarea, that they had been brought to Christ, they summoned Peter to reprimand him for companying with the Gentiles. Peter rehearses the whole matter with them with so much earnestness and truth that they realize that *"forasmuch then as God gave them* (the Gentiles) *the like gift as He did unto us, who believed on the Lord Jesus Christ... they held their peace, and glorified God, saying, 'Then hath God also to the Gentiles granted repentance unto life'"* (vv. 17-18).

They had up to this time been preaching the Word of God only to the Jews. When they, who had been scattered abroad, heard these things concerning the Gentiles they also turned to the Gentiles and great numbers believed and turned onto the Lord. When the church in Jerusalem heard of masses being brought to Christ they sent Barnabas as far as Antioch and he *"exhorted them all, that with purpose of heart they would cleave unto the Lord"* (v. 23). It was in Antioch that the disciples of Christ were first called Christians.

Agabus, a prophet from Jerusalem, came to Antioch to prophesy of a great dearth throughout all the world which was realized in the days of Claudius Caesar. During this time of want the disciples of Christ sought to help one another in their need.

Chapter 12

The Herod of this chapter is the grandson of Herod the Great and son of Aristobulus. He was king of Judea from 37 to 44 A. D. and in order to show favour to the Jews he slew James the apostle and brother of John. When he saw that this pleased the Jews he captured Peter also and no doubt would have slain him but the angel of the Lord freed him and led him out of the prison.

At that same time there was a prayer meeting at John Mark's mother's house when freed Peter arrived and knocked on the door. A little girl named Rhoda answered the door and was so shocked to hear Peter's voice that she ran back into the house to tell the gathering it was Peter; but they did not believe her. Finally they answered the door and to their shock and surprise discovered that it truly was Peter. The James of verse 17 is either the Lord's brother or James the son of Alphaeus.

The end of the chapter gives an account of the haughty Herod accepting the praises of the mob. Josephus says he was arrayed in golden robes and as he stood on the balcony addressing the people the sun glittered off the gold and the people shouted *"it is the voice of a god, and not of a man"* (v. 22). In Herod's acceptance of this blasphemous shout God smote him with a horrible affliction and he died.

Chapter 13

The church in Antioch, according to the guidance of the Holy Ghost, commissioned Paul and Barnabas to go forth to preach the word in regions beyond Jerusalem. When in Paphos, which was on the west coast of Cyprus and was the capital, they came in contact with a sorcerer whose name was Bar-Jesus or Elymas. In verse 9 for the first time we get the name Paul instead of Saul. Paul reproved this man and caused him to be blind. The deputy of Cyprus was a Roman, Sergius Paulus. He was amazed at what had transpired concerning Elymas and *"believed, being astonished at the doctrine of the Lord"* (v. 12).

Paul and his company leave Paphos and go to Perga in Pamphylia and then to Antioch in Pisidia. On the sabbath day they went into the synagogue of the Jews. After the service was ended the rulers of the synagogue asked to hear a word from any of these visiting brethren. Paul stood up and gave a lengthy address which goes from verse 16 to 41. It would seem that there were Gentiles also in attendance at this meeting, which is very strange for in verse 42, 44-45 we read *"And when the Jews were gone out of the synagogue, the Gentiles besought that these words might be preached to them the next Sabbath... and the next Sabbath day came almost the whole city together to hear the word of God. But when the Jews saw the multitudes, they were filled with envy, and spake against those things which were spoken by Paul, contradicting and blaspheming."* Paul makes a most dramatic and judgmental statement to these religious Jews, *"...It was necessary that the Word of God should first have been spoken to you: but seeing ye put it from you, and judge yourselves unworthy of everlasting life, lo, we turn to the Gentiles"* (v. 46). This pleased the Gentiles and they glorified the Word of the Lord. But the Jews stirred up opposition against Paul and his followers and forced them out of the city.

Chapter 14

Next Paul and Barnabas visit Iconium and go into a synagogue there. A great multitude of both Jews and Greeks believed. But the unbelieving Jews stirred up the people against Paul and his accompanying brethren. The city was divided between Paul and the unbelieving Jews. So strong was this opposition that they fled into Lystra and Derbe, cities of Lycaonia.

There was a certain man there, a cripple whom Paul, through the power which God had given him, healed. This man then leapt and walked. This so stunned and amazed the people of the city that they sought to make Paul and Barnabas their gods. Unlike Herod, who had eagerly accepted the plaudits of the people, Paul and Barnabas refused such adoration, declaring *"we also are men of like passions with you"* (v. 15).

Jews came from Antioch and persuaded the people against Paul and Barnabas. The utter fickleness of men's hearts is shown out, for those who only days before had sought to make Paul and Barnabas gods, now take Paul by force out of the city and seek to kill him by stoning him and leaving him as one dead. Many feel that it is of this moment that Paul speaks in 2 Corinthians 12:2. *"I knew a man in Christ above fourteen years ago, whether in the body, I cannot tell: or whether out of the body I cannot tell: God knoweth"*.

But through a miracle of God Paul is resuscitated and stands up on his feet and returns to the city again. The next day they depart to go to Derbe. As they travel throughout the region they ordained elders in all the churches.

Chapter 15

The laws of Judaism with its rituals and rites begins to permeate the church. Paul and Barnabas argue against such influences and because this legalism became so severe it was decided to send a deputation to Jerusalem about the matter of circumcision. And so they journey back to Jerusalem to meet with the apostles and elders.

The legalistic Pharisees insist on circumcision be they Jew or Gentile but Peter stood up before them and said, *"Men and brethren, ye know how that a good while ago God made choice among us, that the Gentiles by my mouth should hear the word of the gospel, and believe"* (v. 7). Christ had given Peter the keys of the kingdom to open this kingdom to both Jew and Gentile (Matt. 16:19). But Peter's specific charge was to be the apostle to the Jews as was Paul's to the Gentiles. Then Paul and Barnabas address the multitude as to the mighty works that God had performed through them. In verse 13 James, no doubt the James of chapter 12:17, stood forth and reviewed God's dealings with the Gentiles.

The apostles and elders are prominent in this chapter. These elders would have been appointed by the apostles by the laying on of hands. It was also decided to send Paul and Barnabas to the Gentiles in Antioch, which had become the centre for Gentile Christians with only four stipulations: that they abstain from pollutions of idols, and from fornication, and from things strangled, and from eating blood (vv. 20, 29).

Verse 33: Paul and Barnabas continue for awhile in Antioch teaching and preaching the word of the Lord. Paul suggests that they go and revisit the areas where they had preached before but Barnabas wished to take John Mark, his nephew, with them. But Paul had been offended by John Mark's actions in Pamphilia and did not wish him to accompany them. Unhappily their arguments were so heated that they parted asunder and Paul chose Silas to go with him. They travelled through Syria and Cilicia encouraging the saints there.

The account of this dissension between Paul and Barnabas reminds me of a story told about the British commander Oliver Cromwell. There were many who wished to paint a portrait of this famous man but he repeatedly refused. Finally he relented but told the artist "you may paint me but with warts and all". The Bible does not try to hide the warts and even such a great spiritual leader as King David has his "warts and all" exposed.

Chapter 16

There are two interesting points to be noticed in this chapter: Timothy is introduced and through the context of words in the chapter we see that Luke the beloved physician, and the writer of this book, joins Paul's company. Through looking at the various verses concerning Timothy in the Bible we learn a good deal about him. He was a young, sickly, meek man whose mother Eunice and grandmother Lois were Jewesses but his father was a Greek. A Jew is counted so through his mother. He was undoubtedly Paul's convert in the faith and Paul looked upon him as his own son.

Timothy became Paul's companion in his labours and often mentions him in conjunction with himself in the work of the Lord. They travelled throughout the Gentile towns and cities encouraging the believers and establishing them in the faith.

While in Mysia they planned to go to Bithynia but the Spirit of God exercised them not to do so. They go to Troas and while there a vision appeared to Paul to encourage him to go to Macedonia. Paul must have walked very close to the Lord to receive these various communications from God.

Please note that the *"they"* of verses 6, 7 turns to *"we"* in verses 10, 13 etc. Luke had joined the little band. They eventually arrive at Philippi which was the chief city of that part of Macedonia. On the Sabbath (Saturday) a company of Christians go to a riverside where it was their practice to pray. Lydia was a seller of purple for which the Phoenicians were famous. The Spirit of God had previously worked in her heart and she received the gospel gladly and was baptized. She persuaded Paul and his company to reside at her house. At this time a young woman possessed with demons harassed Paul by crying out *"These men are the servants of the most high (Elyon) God"* (v. 17). Paul being grieved by this exhorted the evil spirit to come out of her, which it did. Those who had used her for gain were angry with Paul and hauled him before the judges of the city. These followers of Christ were cruelly beaten and thrown into jail. At midnight while singing praises to God, He sent a great earthquake which opened the prison doors and the prisoners' hands were loosed from their bonds. The warden of the jail in a great fright was about to kill himself but Paul spoke words of comfort and hope. The jailer cried out *"what must I do to be saved"*? and Paul replied *"believe on the Lord Jesus Christ, and thou shalt be saved, and thy house"*. (vv. 30, 31). The jailer overjoyed took Paul and his companions to his own home and fed and bedded them for the night.

In the morning the magistrates sent word to the jailer to free them but Paul was indignant and said *"They have beaten us openly… let them come themselves and fetch us out"* (v. 37). And so the magistrates came and brought them out but desired that they would leave their city. And so they said farewell to Lydia and departed.

Chapter 17

Paul's visit to Thessalonica and Athens plays a major part in this chapter. Again the word *"they"* is introduced causing us to believe that Luke was not in this company. Paul and those with him travel to Thessalonica and as it was Paul's custom they went into the synagogue of the Jews. For three Sabbath days Paul reasons with the Jews out of the Scriptures. The unbelieving Jews were incensed by Paul's words and sought to harm him but could not find him. But Jason, of whom we have no record, was taken and reprimanded and let go.

Paul and Silas fled to Berea and went into the synagogue of the Jews. *"These were more noble than those in Thessalonica, in that they received the word with all readiness of mind, and searched the Scriptures daily, whether those things were so"* (v. 11). Were it even so today!

When the Jews of Thessalonica heard of the conversions in Berea they travelled there and stirred up the people. So Paul departed and came to Athens. Paul was greatly moved by the idolatry of that great city. There was a spot in Athens called Mars Hill where intellectuals met to discuss current events. Certain philosophers brought Paul to Areopagus or Mars Hill to hear what new things Paul could tell them.

From verses 21 to 32 Paul most eloquently and with much wisdom brings before them the gods that they ignorantly worshipped. There was a certain amount of subterfuge in this message using quotations from their own poets. The vast knowledge that Paul had acquired of other religions and beliefs is evident here.

There were those who were moved by Paul's message but the three classes of hearers are divided into: those who mocked, those who procrastinated and those who believed. Of which class are you dear reader?

Chapter 18

After leaving Athens Paul journeyed to Corinth. At this point we should say something about the city of Corinth. We shall have more to say when we come to our overview of 1 and 2 Corinthians.

Corinth was basically marked by its high incidence of immorality that had also crept into the churches there. Sad to say to this day the character of the church in a certain city is often coloured or affected by the morals of that city. Corinth was the capital of the province of Achaia. It was a city of wealth brought there by the commercialism of the merchants of that place. It had two harbours and goods were transported there from all over the known world. It was situated on the cross-roads to Italy and Spain to the west and from Asia Minor and Egypt to the east. The immorality of the city was well known and its chief temple was dedicated to Aphrodite, the goddess of love. These worshippers practiced religious prostitution. To Corinthianize meant "to practice sexual immorality".

It was to this immoral city that Paul ventures and stays with Aquila and Priscilla who were of the same craft as Paul, tent makers. While with this faithful couple, who had an assembly in their own home (Rom. 16:3-5) Paul went to the synagogue each Sabbath day and reasoned with the Jews and Greek proselytes.

We are not unfamiliar in reading of these Greeks being in the Jewish synagogues throughout the book of Acts. From the contents in verses 4 to 6 it would seem that these Jews argued and quarrelled with Paul to the point of blasphemy causing Paul finally to proclaim *"Your blood be upon your own heads; I am clean: from henceforth I will go unto the Gentiles"* (v. 6).

But there are those who believed Paul's message of a risen Christ. One was Justus with whom Paul stayed for a while and another was Crispus the chief ruler of the synagogue. After receiving a word from the Lord Paul continued in Corinth for a year and a half.

Again the legalistic Jews, in hatred toward Paul, brought him to the chief deputy of Achaia, Gallio. Gallio would have nothing to do with the Jews' arguments against Paul and had not the least interest in the Jewish religion.

Paul, after spending considerable time at Corinth, left there for Ephesus with Priscilla and Aquila. While there he reasoned with the Jews in their synagogue. They must have had an interest in Paul's message for they urged him to stay, but he said he could not because he wished to be in Jerusalem at the time of a Jewish feast.

When he landed at Caesarea on his way he greeted the church there. It is interesting to see how Paul goes from synagogue to church or assembly. He leaves there and on his journey to Jerusalem stops to minister at various Christian gatherings in Galatia and Phrygia (v. 23).

Verse 24: There was a Jew named Apollos who Paul perhaps met at Phrygia although he was born at Alexandria in Egypt. He is the only person in all Scripture who is spoken of as being eloquent and mighty in the Scriptures. He came to Ephesus and taught diligently the things of the Lord but only knowing up to the baptism of John, the baptism of national repentance. Although he had a Grecian name he was a Jew by birth. It would seem he had heard little of the events concerning Christ and was anticipating the coming of the Messiah. With the knowledge he had from the Old Testament he spoke boldly in the synagogue.

When Aquila and Priscilla heard him they *"expounded unto him the way of God more perfectly"* (v. 26). The order of names for this faithful couple was usually Priscilla and Aquila but when it comes to teaching Aquila is put first.

Chapter 19

This was to be Paul's third and final journey. Paul pays his final visit to Ephesus and visits with certain disciples who in knowledge were very much similar to Apollos. They had been baptized, but unto John's baptism, the baptism of repentance. Paul undoubtedly spoke to them and taught them about Jesus and of His death and resurrection and then they were baptized unto Christ. When Paul laid his hands upon them they received the Holy Ghost. There were twelve disciples (v. 7). Twelve is the number for administration.

For a three month period Paul preached in the synagogue there. Resistance by the legalistic Jews was as stormy here as elsewhere and Paul disputed with them for the space of two years; but this resulted in those who dwelt in Asia in hearing the word of God. Great miracles accompanied Paul as they did Peter. Ephesus was the centre of worship of the goddess Diana. All types of idolatry was practised in that city but the power of

God was manifested against these evils causing many to believe and to toss their evil books onto a common fire. The work of God grew mightily and the power of God prevailed (v. 20).

Paul purposed in his soul to return to Jerusalem. The stirring up of the citizens of Ephesus caused public outcries against Paul and his doctrine. One Demetrius, a silversmith who made his living from making statues of the goddess Diana, gathered his fellow workmen together and troubled them by saying that they were in fear of losing their craft because of Paul. This so troubled these craftsmen that they aroused the whole city against Paul and his companions. They took Gaius and Aristarchus, two of Paul's companions by force. There was great chaos and confusion in the city. They took Alexander of whom we know little, and sought an explanation from him. But when these Gentiles heard him speak in the Jewish tongue they were the more enraged and for two hours cried out *"Great is Diana of the Ephesians"* (v. 34).

A voice of reason is heard above the din and uproar for the town clerk calms the crowd by saying that they should bring the whole matter before the law *"for we are in danger to be called in question for this day's uproar"* (v. 40).

Chapter 20

After this rebellious event Paul leaves for Macedonia and Greece where he stayed for three months. On his return to Macedonia there were many who accompanied him (v. 4). It would appear that Luke had again joined Paul's entourage for the *"us"* and *"we"* are again introduced.

They sailed from Philippi and came to Troas. *"Upon the first day of the week, when the disciples came together to break bread, Paul preached unto them... until midnight"* (v. 7). What important information we have in these few words. The first time we hear of the *"first day of the week"* is in Matthew 28:1 where Mary has come to the sepulchre seeking Jesus. It is repeated in Mark 16:2 and 9, Luke 24:1 and John 20:1, 19 in recording the same occasion. And for the last time in 1 Corinthians 16:2. The reason they came together was to *"break bread"*. These two words are given as though all would understand what was meant. Were the Jewish converts ignorant of the importance and reason for breaking bread? Indeed the custom was not unknown to them for we read in Jeremiah, *"Neither shall men tear themselves for them in mourning* (marginal reading - break bread for them) *to comfort them for the dead; neither shall men give them the cup of consolation to drink for their father or for their mother"* (ch. 16:7).

On this occasion Paul preached until midnight. It would seem from 1 Corinthians 11, that the Lord's supper was held just before or after the saints had a love feast (Jude 12 *"feasts of charity"*), probably before. A young man Eutychus fell asleep and no doubt sitting on the window sill fell out and fell three stories to the ground. The congregation feared that he was dead but Paul, in the fashion of Elijah and Elisha stretched himself upon him and life returned to his body. When they returned to their meeting room they had their meal. William Kelley writes "no doubt it was 'the loaf' of the Lord's supper; but it was that loaf now partaken of by the apostle for his own refreshment" ("The Acts of the Apostles" by Wm Kelley, page 298).

Verse 13: *"And we went before to ship, and sailed unto Assos, there intending to take in Paul"*. We are often left in the dark as to every detail of Paul's travels and visitation, but on the whole Luke is a recorder of minute details.

Paul joins Luke and company and they sailed to Samos for the night, and the next day came to Miletus (v. 15). And from Miletus they travelled to Ephesus and the elders of the church were called together.

Then follows verses 18 to 35 in which Paul gives his great and touching last words to this assembled company in Ephesus. I will not try to detail this wonderful talk for it is plain and heart warming to all who read it.

After Paul had finished they all knelt down and prayed together, no doubt commending their beloved brother to the Lord. How the tears must have flowed. *"Sorrowing most of all... that they should see his face no more"* (v. 38).

Chapter 21

Paul, Luke and the others sailed from Ephesus and eventually came to Tyre, the major seaport of Syria on the extreme east of the Mediterranean. They remained there only three days.

Verse 5 gives us a touching view. As they came to embark the brethren accompanied them with their wives and little ones and they all knelt down on the shore and prayed.

From Tyre they travelled to Caesarea by way of Ptolemais and entered into the house of Philip *"the evangelist"* (v. 8). The same one who had opened the Scriptures to the Ethiopian eunuch and God had opened his eyes. He had four unmarried daughters who were prophetesses (v. 9). That is all it says of them but we can be sure that if a risen Christ had given them this gift He would also have given them the field in which to practice it apart from the assembly meeting.

While they tarried in the house of Philip a certain prophet named Agabus came and in the style of the Old Testament prophets took Paul's girdle and bound his own hands with it. He said, *"Thus saith the Holy Ghost, so shall the Jews at Jerusalem bind the man that owneth this girdle, and shall deliver him into the hands of the Gentiles"* (v. 11).

Paul's great desire to return to Jerusalem and to be with his own people drove him, against many warnings, to return there. We can see this great love he had for his fellow Israelites in Romans 10 and 11. Paul's determination is shown in these words *"I am ready not to be bound only, but also to die at Jerusalem for the name of the Lord Jesus"* (v. 13). And so they go up to Jerusalem.

An elderly disciple named Mnason had a home in Jerusalem and with him Paul lodged. The next day Paul addressed the elders and James, who was the chief of the Jews in Jerusalem, and told them the things God had wrought among the Gentiles and of the many thousands of Jews which had believed the gospel.

Verse 21: *"And they* (the Jews) *are informed of thee, that thou teachest all the Jews which are among the Gentiles to forsake Moses, saying that they ought not to circumcise their children, neither to walk after the customs"*. Was not this the very thing that had so incensed the Jews (ch. 6:11)? The word *"forsake"* is in the original "apostatize" and is also found in 2 Thessalonians 2:3.

The company of elders persuaded Paul to submit to a Jewish ritual. This seems out of character for Paul and goes against his own words (Gal. 2:3-5). We must leave the estimation of his actions to the judgment seat of Christ. We can be sure of one thing; Paul's whole heart was to honour Christ.

When the seven days of purification were almost ended Paul was spotted in the Temple and a great outcry was made by the people against him. They took Paul and drew him out of the Temple and sought to kill him such was their hatred toward him (vv. 30-31). The local Roman authority intervened to save Paul's life and to calm the mob. As Paul was being led into the castle he spoke unto the chief captain in Greek. Paul asked for licence to speak to the multitude and when this was permitted he spoke to them in the Hebrew tongue which quieted the group.

Chapter 22

In this chapter we have recorded another of Paul's speeches of which we find many in the book of Acts. Paul gives a brief biography and for the second time records his conversion on the road to Damascus. Each time the light becomes brighter. He once again repeats God's desire for him that he would be God's messenger to the Gentiles. When Paul uses the word *"Gentile"* (v. 21), there was such a hatred toward them by the Jews, that they sought to kill Paul. But the chief captain intervened and for the safety of Paul brought him into the safety of the castle. Before he was scourged he made known that he was a Roman by birth and this so shocked the military personnel that they loosed Paul from his bonds and brought him before the Council of officials and dignitaries and religious rulers.

Chapter 23

We are told in this chapter that the council was not only composed of Gentile rulers and Jewish priests but members of the Pharisees and Sadducees were present. The one party was in opposition to the other. Paul uses this knowledge to set one against the other. Through this ruse there arose a great discussion among them and in fear that Paul might have been slain the chief captain intervened and whisked Paul to the castle.

In their hatred toward Paul certain Jews banded together with the purpose to kill him. This murderous plan was made known to the chief priests and elders. It would appear that these religious legalists sought to go ahead with this plan (v. 15).

But Paul's nephew heard of this and he carried the news to his uncle. Paul told a centurion to take his nephew to the chief captain to tell him of this conspiracy. The nephew told the chief captain of all that he had heard. He called unto him two centurions to prepare an army of two hundred soldiers plus horsemen and spearmen to escort Paul in safety to Felix the governor with a letter. Claudius Lysias, for that was the chief captain's name, recorded the past events to Felix in this letter.

So this army took Paul to Caesarea. When Felix had read the letter and when he found out that Paul was of the province of Cilicia he said, *"I will hear thee...when thine accusers are also come"* (v. 35) and so Paul was imprisoned in Herod's judgment hall.

Chapter 24

In five days time Ananias the high priest and the elders came with a certain lawyer named Tertullus to accuse Paul before the council. Tertullus claimed Paul had done many profane things in Jerusalem and the temple there. After Tertullus' condemnation of Paul he was allowed to speak on his own behalf. Paul recounts his sojourn in Jerusalem and the Jews opposition to him.

When Felix had heard these words from Paul he put off his judgment until his successor Festus should come. The avariciousness of the man can be seen by his desire of bribe money from Paul.

Chapter 25

When Festus had come from Caesarea to take up his new appointment the leaders of the Jews informed him of their accusations against Paul and desired him to take Paul to Jerusalem so they could murder him on the way. But Festus kept Paul at Caesarea and after ten days went there himself.

Once more a council is brought together to bring their many false charges against Paul. Paul seeks once more to answer to these charges. Festus asked Paul if he was willing to go to Jerusalem to be judged whereupon Paul appealed to be judged by no less than Caesar to which Festus agreed.

A few days later Agrippa and his sister Bernice came to Caesarea to honour Festus on his appointment. Festus makes known the facts to Agrippa as he understood them. Agrippa replied that he wished to hear Paul for himself. So the next day Paul is brought once more before an auspicious company.

Chapter 26

Agrippa gives Paul the liberty to answer for himself before this council. Paul reviews his former life as a Pharisee and a persecutor of the people of "the way" and his conversion on the road to Damascus. Verse 17 is to be noted for we read that Paul was to be an evangelist to the Gentiles (also v. 20). Paul clearly proclaims the gospel before all in verse 23.

Festus, no doubt agitated by Paul's words, cried out *"much learning doth make thee mad"* (v. 24). Paul turns to Agrippa who had been visibly moved by Paul's defense and said, *"King Agrippa, believest thou the prophets? I know that thou believest"* (v. 27). Whereupon Agrippa replied, *"Do you think that in such a short time you can persuade me to be a Christian?"* (v. 28, NIV). Paul's gracious answer endears us to this faithful apostle, *"I would to God, that not only thou, but also all that hear me this day, were both almost, and altogether such as I am, except these bonds"* (v. 29).

Their judgment on this matter was that if Paul had not appealed to Caesar he would have been freed.

Chapters 27 & 28

The next two remarkable chapters tell us of Paul's dangerous sea journey to Rome. The repetitions of the word *"we"* shows us that Luke was with Paul on this fateful journey.

Because these two chapters have been much written upon, I will not go into detail here except to say that Luke's great intelligence and particular ability to record great detail cannot be missed. It has been said by many that the details of the sea journey and the inclement weather and the details of the ship and its cargo, at this period of time, has not been surpassed in all literature. How much different this saga would have been recorded had the apostle Peter, say, been the writer. Once again God had the right man at the right time and place to record this amazing story.

For myself one verse stands out from the pages of these two chapters. *"Sirs, be of good cheer: for I believe God"* (v. 25). This great faith of Paul is what kept him and gave him strength, wisdom and courage. After many dangerous experiences and a tremendous shipwreck on an island called Mileta (Malta), Paul and the other prisoners embarked on another ship headed for Syracuse on the island of Scila part of the southern tip of Italy. There were brethren waiting for Paul and after seven days they departed for Rome.

Along the way various Christians greeted Paul and company and encouraged them on their way. I wonder what effect all this had on the Roman guardians who were escorting Paul to Rome. They could not help but be affected.

When Paul had suitably rested, after three days, he called the chief of the Jews together and explained the reason for his coming to Rome to be tried.

Rome was not Jerusalem but many hundreds of miles distance. What was common knowledge in Palestine had been little heard of in Rome. The Jews in Rome knew little of the doctrines of Christianity, "this sect" as they called it. And so a day was appointed in which Paul expounded to the Jews from their own Scripture about Jesus. These meetings were intense and we can imagine with what fervour Paul preached Christ and Him crucified from morning until evening. But to what avail were Paul's words; for some believed and some did not. Could we not say that after all of Paul's trials, experiences and dangers, and with much passionate love for his own people and after speaking faithfully to these Jews of Rome, that their refusal to accept the good seed was a tremendous frustration to Paul.

These final verses (vv. 25-26, 28) are a precursor to the following Epistles by Paul to the Gentiles. *"Well spake the Holy Ghost by Esaias* (Isaiah) *the prophet unto our fathers, saying, go unto this people, and say, hearing ye shall hear, and shall not understand; and seeing ye shall see, and not perceive... Be it known therefore unto you, that the salvation of God is sent unto the Gentiles, and that they will hear it."* In Romans 11:11 we read, *"Through their* (Israel's) *fall salvation is come unto the Gentiles"*.

Conclusion

God's ways are beyond our understanding. We Gentiles who were but strangers to the covenants and the promises of God to Israel are now brought into the full liberty of sons through the setting aside of Israel for a time.

> God could not pass the sinner by,
> His sins demands that He must die;
> But in the cross of Christ we see
> How God can save, yet righteous be.
>
> —Albert Midlane

"Thanks be unto God for this unspeakable gift"(2 Cor. 9:15). Amen and Amen.

THE EPISTLE OF PAUL THE APOSTLE TO THE *Romans*

Introduction

As the Acts of the Apostles give us the history of the founding of Christianity, so Romans gives us the doctrines upon which this new faith was founded. The followers of Christ were first called Christians at Antioch (Acts 11:26). The faith spread as persecution came for as the saying goes, "the blood of the martyrs is the seed of the church." The only other time the word "Christian" is used in the Bible is in Acts 20:28 when Agrippa said to Paul *"almost thou persuadest me to be a Christian."*

Chapters 1 *&* 2

Luke, the beloved physician and companion of Paul, wrote a second treatise to his friend Theophilus, which we know as the Acts of the Apostles to explain the history of this new faith. Paul was the apostle chosen of God to write and spread the truth of the gospel of Jesus Christ to the Gentiles.

The saints in Rome were much to be praised, for their faith in the gospel had been spread abroad throughout the whole world (ch. 1:8). Though he had never seen them nor visited Rome, Paul wished to impart to them *"some spiritual gift, to the end ye may be established"* (v. 11). He begins by telling them that this gospel (good news) *"is the power (dynamos) of God unto salvation to every one that believeth; to the Jew first, and also to the Greek"* (v. 16). Faith in Christ is the only key that unlocks the door to Christianity (v. 17). It is important to notice that it is to the Jew first. In the first three chapters Paul establishes the fact that the whole world is guilty before God, *"for all have sinned, and come short of the glory of God"* (ch. 3:23). In chapter 1 the barbarian is brought before us. In chapter two the Greek. In the first section of chapter two we have the moral Gentile with a conscience which told him when he did wrong but could not give him the power to stop. Then beginning in verse 17 of chapter two we have a picture of the legal Jew. Paul draws on Old Testament Scriptures when reproaching these legalistic Jews, for they knew the Scriptures.

Chapter 3

Paul quotes from the Old Testament to emphasize his conclusion on all types of men, moral or immoral, Jew or Gentile, that *"all have sinned, and come short of the glory of God."* (ch.3:23), and that there is none righteous in any of these classes (ch. 3:10-11).

Chapter 4

Paul pits faith against works. Of what value is the death of Christ if we are saved by our good works? We are told in Isaiah that all our works are as filthy rags (Isaiah 64:6). Paul repeats the word *"faith"* 10 times in this chapter to emphasize his point. The keeping of the law only works wrath (ch. 4:15). Verse 21 gives us a good definition of faith. *"And being fully persuaded that, what He had promised, He was able also to perform."* What does a poor unregenerate man need to do then?

Chapter 5

This chapter gives us the answer; we are justified not by the law but by faith in a risen Christ. The 5th chapter is a summation of the first four. The words *"much more"* are used in verses 9, 15, 17 and 20 emphasizing that through faith in Christ salvation abounds unto righteousness and is the only entrance into the kingdom of God. Up to verse 12 of chapter 5 the Word is dealing with the question of sin; after verse 12 the nature that produced those sins. *"We are justified by faith."* We cannot add more to this nor subtract from it.

In this chapter we are presented with two heads of the races, Adam and Christ. In chapter 6 we have two masters, sin and Christ. In chapter seven we have two husbands, Christ and the law. Christ predominates in every case.

Chapter 6

We must accept the truth that the old man has been put to death in and through the death of Christ. *"Know ye not, that so many of us as were baptized into Jesus Christ were baptized into His death?"* (v. 3). Our old man is crucified with Him (v. 6) and now we walk in newness of life for as we are buried with Him we also are raised with Him. The Christian is seen in an entirely new standing: *"old things are passed away; behold, all things are become new"* (2 Cor. 5:17). He automatically becomes the child of another country. We are no longer under the law, for Christ has become the end of the law, for us He fulfilled the law in every aspect. We are now under grace (v. 14).

Chapter 7

It has been well said that when we receive Christ we are saved but when we trust His Word we are safe. This is an important point. The one in this chapter has not taken God at His word and though saved is miserable (v. 24.) It has been said that as believers we need to get out of chapter 7 and into chapter 8. When we accept unconditionally the truth that we have been delivered from sin and Christ is now our life; when we realize the old man can do nothing to please God and we put that life in the place of death; when we are brought intelligently into the liberty of being saved then we are safe. *"In whom also after that ye believed, ye were sealed with that Holy Spirit of promise"* (Eph. 1:13).

Chapter 8

Paul puts the stamp of the approval of God on our faith in this chapter. All that has gone before is rectified in this first verse *"there is therefore now no condemnation to them which are in Christ Jesus."* The latter part of this verse is not in the original but is rightly put in verse 4.

If one gets hold of this, his conscience has peace and rest with God. The law cannot save but only condemns us. Christ came to fulfil the law and thus put an end to it for man. The Spirit of God dwells in us (v. 9). The spirit in man is the God conscious part of our being. Every believer has the Spirit of God dwelling in him. This is not the same as being filled with the Spirit. *"Hope"* in this chapter (vv. 23-25) is delayed certainty.

We believers have been brought unto the glorious liberty of sons (v. 21) *"whereby we cry, Abba, Father"* (v. 15). We are joint heirs with Christ (vv. 14-17). We are now seen by God in all the righteousness of Christ. Though we were once the enemies of God (ch. 5:6, 8 and 10) now nothing can separate us from the love of God (ch. 8:38-39).

Chapters 9, 10 & 11

These chapters are a parenthesis which give us Paul's great concern for his Jewish brethren. The general theme of sin and salvation for lost man we have read of in chapters 1 to 8. Now we begin the second section: Paul's great desire was to see his own fellow Jews brought to Christ. He, like Moses, was willing to be cut off from God for his brethren in the flesh (v. 3). The Jew sought salvation by the keeping of the law, but this only condemned him and promised death for it was impossible for him, or any man, to keep the whole law (vv. 31-32).

Chapter 10

Chapter 10 continues Paul's discourse in regard to his people. The Jew sought righteousness through the keeping of the law but Christ is the end of the law for righteousness to every one that believeth. The law may be used by God to bring a man to Christ but when he comes he finds that Christ died in his place and has become his righteousness before God. A much used gospel verse is found in verse 9.

Chapter 11

This chapter concerns the Jews and the Gentiles. The church is but a parenthesis in the ways of God. When the church is caught home at the Rapture then all God's purposes and prophesies concerning Israel will come into force. The times of the Gentiles will be over. Yet God has preserved within the church's body a remnant of Jews according to the election of grace (v. 5). It was through the fall of Israel that righteousness has been brought to the Gentiles (v. 11). Blindness in part has happened to Israel; there is a veil over their eyes which shall be taken away when one comes to Christ (2 Cor. 3:14-16).

Chapter 12

Chapter 12 gives us guidance for the individual's conduct in the assembly or church. The individual in the church is to understand his gift and service and seek to nurture this and exercise it for the benefit and blessing of all (1 Tim. 4:15). The giving of gifts is the subject of three chapters in the New Testament. In Romans 12 these gifts are given by God to the assembly (v. 3), *"as God hath dealt to every man."* The gifts listed here (vv. 6-8) are numerous, more than the other two portions. There are, not surprisingly, seven gifts mentioned and they are for the assembly. No evangelist is named.

In 1 Corinthians 12 gifts are given by the Spirit of God (v. 4, 9, 11). Again the evangelist is left out, for 1 Corinthians contains truth for the church. Verse 9 gives us the particular gifts. (Note, they are all for the church).

In Ephesians we are seen seated with Christ in the heavenlies and therefore it is fitting that the gifts here are given by an ascended Christ to the church. *"But unto every one of us is given grace according to the measure of the gift of Christ"* (Eph. 4:7). It is of interest to note that in Psalm 68:18 which is quoted in Ephesians 4:8 Christ received gifts for men. In Ephesians 4 He gives those gifts unto men (v. 8).

And so we see from these three portions that the whole Trinity is involved in these gifts to the church.

Chapter 13

This chapter gives us guidance for the individual's conduct in the world. We are to submit to the powers that be for they are ordained of God. God has set men in authority to preserve law and order. At times these may be the basest of men (Dan. 4:17). Psalm 82 speaks of these judges (gods) and their expected conduct. But there is a higher power, for God ruleth in the kingdom of men. Such things as, respecting authority, paying taxes, tribute to whom tribute is due etc. (vv. 6-8) are right and proper.

Chapters 14 & 15

Chapters 14 and 15 compare those who are weak to those who are strong. The weak are those who, though saved, have never removed themselves from living under the law. These individuals are still living under the law and its ordinances. But those who are strong are those who walk in the liberty wherein Christ has set them free (Rom. 3:24) and do so as sons not as servants (1 Cor. 8:9-13). Chapter 7 presents one such who is miserable because he has never come to the realization that Christ came and fulfilled the law and set him free from it (Col. 2:12-18).

Chapter 16

This chapter along with Hebrews 11, has been called God's honour roll. Phebe was a sister, a servant of the church. Philip had *"four daughters, virgins which did prophesy"* (Acts 21:9). God never gives a gift to an individual whether man or woman that He doesn't intend for it to be used. Women have been used of God in thousands of incidents but God has ruled that they are not to speak in the assembly (1 Cor. 14:34). The Lord has His reasons for this and we must be obedient to His Word.

Priscilla and Aquila were tent makers and for a time Paul laboured with them. The assembly met in their house. (v. 5).

After this list of faithful believers is given, Paul warns us to beware of those who come among us who cause divisions or teach contrary to the doctrine of Christ (1 John 2:19, 3 John 9-10).

Conclusion

Paul only wrote a few epistles with his own hand, perhaps because of his failing eyesight.*"See what large letters..."* (Gal. 6:11, NIV). Others wrote down what he dictated. Tertius, who we know little of, wrote this epistle.

If you would wish to know of the revelation of the mystery which was kept secret since the world began, turn to Ephesians 3:1-8 and Colossians 1:25-27.

THE *First* EPISTLE OF PAUL THE APOSTLE TO THE *Corinthians*

Introduction

Corinth, in the apostle Paul's day, was the Las Vegas of the east "Sin City". It was the crossroads between the east and the west. Wherever there is the fleshly quality of love, the eros, one will find lasciviousness of every kind. The worship of one of the forms of a female goddess prevailed, Aphrodite, and sexual pleasures of every form were practiced by the population and in the temples. The name Corinth became a byword for anyone who was lewd and sexual. The word *"Korinthiazoinai"* attached to any person meant that he led a debauched life.

It was in this atmosphere that the assembly in Corinth met. Sad to say that assemblies of Christians are often affected by the character of the city in which they dwell and the evils of that city at times permeate the assembly.

This was the case at Corinth in Paul's days. A brother in the assembly had sexual relations with his father's wife and the assembly had ignored it. Paul had received this shocking news from the house of Chloe (ch. 1:11) and to correct this situation, by the power vested in him by God, Paul writes to exercise them to action; to put this wicked person out of fellowship. But there were other reasons which are found in (2 Cor. 7:12). *"Though I wrote unto you, I did it not for his cause that had done the wrong, nor for his cause that suffered wrong, but that our care for you in the sight of God might appear unto you."*

Paul had visited Corinth a number of times (2 Cor. 12:14, 13:1)and it would appear that he was used of God to establish an assembly there. *"Do we begin again to commend ourselves? Or need we, as some others, epistles of commendation to you, or letters of commendation from you? Ye are our epistle written in our hearts, known and read of all men." (2 Cor. 3:1-2).*

But apart from all that pertains to this evil that was being overlooked by the assembly at Corinth there was another great reason for the Spirit of God inspiring Paul to write this epistle. For what we find in the first epistle is the only place in the New Testament where we are given explicit instructions on the conduct of a Christian assembly and the manner in which we are to approach God.

This portion fills the heart of the epistle and is from chapter 10:15 to the end of chapter 14.

The Old Testament is filled with instructions on how we are to approach God but in the New Testament we only find this in the portion specified above. This is to me of major importance and we do well to study and lay to our hearts this most important section (1 Cor. 10:15 to 14:40)

Assembly Order

This portion (ch. 10:15 to 14:40) is equivalent to all the chapters in the Old Testament that instruct Israel on how to approach God. Much of Exodus, Leviticus, and Deuteronomy are taken up with this important subject.

God has His way and man devises many other ways to approach Him. In many ways the New Testament is the antithesis of the Old Testament e.g. the priest in the Old Testament was to have his head covered with the mitre; in the New Testament man is to uncover his head in the presence of God.

The phrase *"holy things"* is repeated many times in the Old Testament, particularly in Leviticus 22. Strangely, it is only used in 1 Corinthians 9:13 in the New Testament; I believe the instruction given in our chapters in Corinthians is in this spirit. We may argue about specifics in regard to head coverings, the breaking of the bread etc., but the spirit of the words should be understood. The minute we start questioning the intent of the teaching of the Spirit of God, we are in trouble (Ezek. 44:8).

The whole subject begins with these words: *"I speak as to wise men; judge ye what I say"* (10:15). To hear God speak to us and learn from Him, we must be humble; *"with the lowly is wisdom"* (Prov. 11:2b). The Holy Spirit would assume we will be wise and hearken. Israel's gross failure was that they would not listen. The subject ends with *"but if any man be ignorant, let him be ignorant"* (14:38). What a sad indictment! If we will not hearken then He will leave us in our ignorance.

The third important verse is found between the two above; *"If any man seem to be contentious* (argumentative), *we have no such custom"* (11:16). It is the Spirit that teaches; we take what He teaches and accept it as truth, there is too much talk today among Christians as to what words mean and the interpretations. It is just in the last decades that we have seen this evil appearing; it is the Spirit that teaches and He never teaches wrongly (1 John 2:27). As soon as our natural minds begin to question about words or expressions that our forefathers in the faith taught as truth for centuries, then we are arguing against the teaching of the Spirit. I wonder what is the purpose of those who do so? Thereby they confuse the saints and cause them to begin questioning other Scriptures.

The subject of the Lord's Table begins with chapter 10:16. Here we have the Lord's Table, **the place**. The cup is mentioned first because our only title to be there is the blood of Christ (Mark 14:23-24). In contrast, 1 Corinthians 11:23-26 is **the act** of breaking bread in communion and so the bread is put first. I think the expression *"the Lord's table"* is only found here (ch. 10:21) in the New Testament and only twice in the Old Testament (Mal. 1:7, 12).

Order seems to be the predominant thought, as well as obedience and subjection; two things that are hateful to man in the flesh. Paul gives us the Lord's commandments and we are to bow to them (14:37). Christ's resurrection has brought in a whole new order of things. Sometimes the Old Testament instruction is given for types and at other times, it is in contrast. The whole subject concludes with *"Let all things be done decently and in order"* (14:40). *"And the rest will I set in order when I come"* (11:34). Projecting this to the Lord's coming, there are serious miscarriages of God's clear instruction for which we must answer. How can we say we love God if we do not keep His Word? (John 14:21). (Note word "*commandments*") **Love is not the love of Christ if obedience and fidelity to God's Word is not observed**. Yes we Christians do have commandments from the Lord, but not in the sense of judicial enforcement as in the Old Testament, but rather the act of loving obedience because of what Christ has done; commandments, not as to a servant, but as to a loving wife.

Chapter 1

Paul was called by God to be the apostle to the Gentiles; we are called by God to be saints. And this is not to be an exclusive gathering of believers but to "*all that in every place call upon the name of Jesus Christ our Lord, both theirs and ours*" (v. 2). I thank God with all my heart for this verse. The body of Christ comprises every believer in every place at all times. It is evil to speak against any Christian organization who believe the Bible to be the Word of God and who worship Him in spirit and in truth. They all are God's children for whom Christ died. And like Thumper in the children's story "Bambi" we can repeat "if you can't say anything nice then say nothing at all."

The house of Chloe did not, through fear of reprisal, stand behind anonymity, but told Paul of the evil being allowed (ch. 1:11). So often those who carry tales do not wish to have their names used.

Chapter 2

Paul had visited Corinth numerous times and did not wish to become embroiled in the schismatic way of these brethren. "*For I determined not to know anything among you, save Jesus Christ, and Him crucified*" (v. 2). Some were saying they were of Paul and others of Apollo, causing strife and division among them (ch. 3:3-7).

There was much gift at Corinth. Paul establishes this immediately in his letter, "*so that ye come behind in no gift*". But theses schisms were tearing them apart.

This chapter gives reference once again to 2 Corinthians 12:6. Paul's physical problems: his speech (vv. 3-4), his bodily presence (2 Cor. 10:1, 10) and his eyesight (Gal. 4:15, 6:11), *"Ye see how large a letter"*. Verse 9: Once again Paul gives us an example of the use of an Old Testament verse being applied in a way to fit the theme. This quote from Isaiah 64:4 does not have the added words *"but God hath revealed them to us by His Spirit"*. The Holy Spirit was given to open to us the mind of God. Those mysteries which were hid for ages have now been revealed to us (Col. 1:26, Eph. 1:9).

Verses 11 to 16: The youngest believer has more wisdom in the things of the Spirit than the wisest unsaved man. We must have the Spirit of God to understand the things of God.

Chapter 3

Though the Corinthian saints had much gift, there was the spirit of carnality among them. There was envying, strife and division. Paul seeks to press upon them that it was God alone, working often behind the scenes, that brought in blessing. How much division has been brought into assemblies because we become attached and followers of some charismatic and outstanding man!

The assembly as the temple of God is once again pressed upon them (2 Cor. 6:16). It is a dangerous thing for the individual to bring in division among God's people (Prov. 6:19). Paul refers to himself as a wise master builder (v. 10). Let us each one be careful and prayerful as to our influence upon the assembly and to God's people in general.

Chapter 4

Oh! the importance of verse 5. So many believers are confused by exactly what will transpire at the judgment seat of Christ. There are a number of judgment seats in the Bible (2 Cor. 5:10, Rev. 20:11-13, Matt. 25:31). But the matter is all made clear when we understand that this judgment seat for the believers is the bema seat, the seat upon which the Greek judges of the athletic games sat to hand out prizes. It is the "reward seat". Dear fellow believer God is finished with the judgment of our sins; Christ answered to this at Calvary's cross when He cried *"it is finished."* There is a false premise circulating that as David's sins were all opened to us in the Scripture so we shall have all ours opened before our brethren in the glory. How distasteful and dishonouring to our God to think so. Did the Lord Jesus openly rebuke Peter for his sin in denying him with oaths and cursing? No, He had a secret meeting with Peter when, I am sure, the Lord dealt with him most graciously and in private. I love the words of Mark chapter 16:7 *"Go your way, tell His disciples **and Peter** He goeth before you into Galilee"*. *"**And Peter**"*. This is the way of my Saviour and my Lord. We shall perhaps write more of this bema seat when we come to 2 Corinthians.

It would seem from verses 7 and 8 that the Corinthian saints lived a rather luxurious life. Paul compares his position as God's servant to these saints who had all the comforts of this world. But as a father feels toward his children, so Paul felt toward these believers.

Chapter 5

Now Paul comes to the point of his reason for writing this letter. A believer in the assembly at Corinth had committed adultery with his father's wife and the Corinthian saints were in such a weakened and carnal condition that they had neither the spirituality nor power to judge the matter. Dear brethren, has such a condition been unknown to you in this present day of worldliness and luxury. Paul with the authority given to him of the Lord Jesus commands these saints to put this wicked person out of the assembly. *"Purge out therefore the old leaven, that ye may be a new lump, as ye are unleavened. For even Christ our passover is sacrificed for us"* (v. 7). Here the type of the Passover is made plain. Christ is our Passover. He, the Paschal Lamb, has been sacrificed for us. *"And when I see the blood, I will **pass over** you"* (Ex. 12:13).

Chapter 6

There are two distinct forms of judgment spoken of in the New Testament: personal judgment of our fellow Christian (Jas.

4:12, Rom. 14:4, Matt. 7:1-5), and assembly judgment. As to the former we are warned not to prejudge our fellow believer, as to the latter the assembly is instructed to judge what needs judging amongst them.

Verse 1. We are distinctly told not to go to the law with our brother in Christ. Better to allow ourselves to be defrauded than to do so. Paul strongly criticizes the saints at Corinth, *"Is it so, that there is not a wise man among you"* (v. 5) ? Did they not realize that they, in no time, would judge the world and the angels? Could they not judge those matters in the assembly?

From verses 9 to 10 a very solemn list is given of those who shall not inherit the kingdom of God. It would do each of us well to read carefully over this list. The word "effeminate" in verse 9 is translated *"those who make women of themselves"* (N. T.). Perhaps in our former lost and unsaved condition some of us performed these evil acts. But now we are washed and set apart for God and justified by Christ. We are new creatures in Christ.

Verse 15. As chapter 3:16 speaks of the assembly as being the temple of God, this portion speaks of the individual as being so. We are joined to the Lord and we are one spirit. The only sin that is spoken of that is against our own bodies is the sin of fornication. How can we take that which is joined to Christ and join it to a harlot? This portion and chapter 7 has to do with fornication, adultery and the marriage state.

Chapter 7

Paul now gives his advice concerning the relationship between a man and a woman. It is well for every young Christian to read this portion carefully. God's moral standards do not change from dispensation to dispensation. We are living in such an immoral, lewd world and the abuse of sexual pleasures is rampant all around us day after day. The young are bombarded with enticements of every description. We are told by God *"be ye holy; for I am holy"* (1 Pet. 1:16), and *"keep thyself pure"* (1 Tim. 5:22).

There are those who need not marry (Matt. 19:12). But at the very beginning God said *"it is not good that the man should be* alone" (Gen. 2:18). And so Paul gives his advice that rather than burn (with desire) it is better to marry (v. 9).

Verses 13 to 14. If one partner in a marriage is a believer, the other is sanctified by him or her and the children are considered holy. It is not childhood baptism that brings them unto holy ground but the fact that the child's father or mother is a believer.

We live our lives as Christians in the liberty in which Christ has set us free. We are not under bondage. Verse 15 bears this out as also in 1 Corinthians 10:27. If we are invited to a feast by an unbeliever the Spirit of God gives us the liberty as to whether or not we should go. I repeat we are not under bondage and are ungirded priests. There are times when God leaves us to *"work out our own salvation with fear and trembling"* (Phil. 2:12).

I will not go into the details of this chapter concerning a man and his sweetheart and a man and his wife, but it should be an obligatory reading for every couple planning to marry.

Chapter 8

This chapter concerns details as to things offered to idols and our concern for our weak brethren. Romans 14 and 15 have much information concerning those who are weak and those who are strong. A weak brother is a newly converted Christian who has not been able to give up his legalistic ways, one who is as the one in Romans chapter 7, he is not able to extricate himself from being under the law.

The danger for us in North America in eating things offered to idols is not nearly as great as it is in some other countries, e.g. India. But the principle of not offending our weaker brother, perhaps one newly come to the faith, still applies. *"Wherefore, if meat* (or any other thing) *make my brother to offend, I will eat no flesh while the world standeth, lest I make my brother to offend"* (v. 13).

Verse 3. *"But if any man love God, the same is known of Him."* The Lord appreciates our love for Him and He honours it. He has a special love for such. *"I love them that love Me; and those that seek Me early shall find Me"* (Prov. 8:17).

Chapter 9

Paul presents his credentials, as it were, for his apostleship. He admits in having been *"one born out of due time"*(1 Cor. 15:8, an abortive). He had seen the Lord and been given His commission by Him. In much of 2 Corinthians he verifies this call by an ascended Christ. *"Are they Hebrews? So am I. Are they Israelites? So am I. Are they the seed of Abraham? So am I. Are they ministers of Christ? (I speak as a fool) I am more; in labours more abundant, in stripes above measure, in prisons more frequent, in deaths oft"* (2 Cor. 11:22-28).

In Philippians, (ch. 3:4-6) Paul tells of what he was and had been. He was a religious zealot and persecuted the believers; he stood and watched Stephen being stoned to death (Act 7:58).

There are seven prides found in this portion in Philippians: pride of nationhood, *"of the stock of Israel"*; pride of family, *"of the tribe of Benjamin"*; pride of race, *"an Hebrew of the Hebrews"*; pride of sect, *"as touching the law, a Pharisee"*; pride of zeal and pride of works, *"persecuting the church"*; pride of keeping the law, *"touching the righteousness which is in the law, blameless"*.

At the heart of this chapter are Paul's words concerning ministering. *"Who goeth a warfare any time at his own charges? Who planteth a vineyard, and eateth not of the fruit thereof? or who feedeth a flock, and eateth not of the milk of the flock?"* (v. 7). But Paul would not have the saints at Corinth think that he was looking for a handout for himself (v. 15). Paul laboured with his own hands, for he was a tentmaker, in order to earn his bread (Acts 18:3, 1 Cor. 4:12, Acts 20:34).

Paul sought, in order to win souls, to make of himself all things to all men. Personally I have thought that this is not always wise as it might get us into trouble and problems. A case in point is found in Acts 21. In order to please his brethren Paul shaved his head and took a vow with the other Jews.

This seems to me to be giving in to the same thing that he withstood Peter to the face about. (Gal. 2:11-16). *"For if I build again the things which I destroyed, I make myself a transgressor"* (Gal. 2:18).

Chapter 10

From verses 1 to 11 Paul reviews Israel's failures in the wilderness and the important type of the rock, so often mentioned in the Old Testament, is made clear *"and that Rock was Christ,"* (Deut. 32:4, 13, 15, 18, 30, 31, 37; Ps. 62:2,6-7; Isaiah 32:2; etc.).

"Now all these thing happened unto them for ensamples: and they are written for our admonition, upon whom the ends of the world (ages) are come" (v. 11). This verse is extremely important. The Old Testament is the picture book for the New. The remarkable types and examples given to us in the Old Testament help us to understand the teachings of the New. An old saw says "the Old is the New concealed, while The New is the Old revealed." These examples are giving us the wisdom not to commit the same sins and failures that Israel fell into. We must bow our heads in shame for I fear the church at large has not benefited from these examples. Beloved brethren let us pay heed to what we read in the Old Testament that we do not fail as a corporate body in the same way Israel did in the wilderness.

And now we come to the great and important section of this book. From chapter 10 verse 15 to the end of chapter 14 we have instructions as to the assembly. As I have given this portion in the first part of this exposition I will not repeat it again.

Chapter 11

Before Paul gives instruction as to the precious remembrance of the Lord, verses 23-24, he gives a little test as to our subjection. The key verse is verse 3. *"The head of Christ is God"*; in everything Jesus was subject and obedient to His Father's word. It is unthinkable that He would ever question God's word or direction. Our head is Christ and have we been as faithful in carrying this out? I fear not.

This whole subject of head covering has become a bone of contention and I believe it is because, like Israel, we want to be like the nations (churches) about us. H.E.H. used to say that "man is a slave to public opinion" and this is true with God's people as well. Why has this spirit manifested itself so much in the last days. (2 Kings 17:33, 1 Sam. 8:5 and 20, Ex. 33:5). *"That we also may be like all the nations."* We seem clear as to head coverings for men but not for women. What would we think if a brother wore a hat during meetings?

Now I repeat that what we have presented here is a small test of our subjection. The **letter** of the words should not be the important thing but rather **the spirit** of what is said (2 Cor. 3:6). To argue, when and on what occasions, a woman is to wear a head covering and a man is not is to lose sight of the force of what the Spirit is seeking to convey. That is why I earlier wrote about **"The Holy Things"**. It seemed to me that Paul is telling us that when we are occupied with the Lord's Word or those things pertaining to Christ and His word we are occupied with "holy things" and we show our subjection and obedience to Him by carrying out His instruction. Many brothers that I have known when they spoke about the Lord whether in their cars or elsewhere would remove their hats. Sisters would cover their heads when Bible reading or prayer was in the house. This is considered "out of style" or "old fashioned". We need to remember also that a woman's hair is her glory and when we meet we want to be occupied with the Lord's glory.

Verse 17 to 22 are historical of what disorder was transpiring at Corinth in the assembly because God's order was not being carried out.

Verse 23 to 34. The act of breaking bread and instruction and warning. I feel verse 30 does not just apply to the one who so sins but other innocent persons may suffer because of one person's being *"guilty of the body and blood of the Lord"* (v. 27).

Chapter 12

It has been said many times that chapter 12 presents the mechanism of the assembly.

Chapter 13

With shame we should bow our heads for having left our first love. The epitome, the base, the core, the reason for all we do should be divine love. Even in writing this I hope I have said these things because I love my brethren and I desire to see them walking in the truth. The rod only drives men deeper into the forest. Verse 4 – What divine love does. Verse 5, 6 – What it does not. Note verse 2 – *"Though I have **all faith**... and have not charity (divine love), I am nothing"*.

Edification is the reason for all that goes on in the assembly. Verse 3 – building up, stirring up, binding up. Now there is some confusion as to tongues in the King James translation. Speaking in tongues exalts self where as one word spoken in the Spirit exalts Christ. I can agree with verse 24 which would annul verse 22. What profit would there be for an unsaved man to come into the assembly and be confounded by tongues and yet if one prophesied it could reach the heart and conscience of the hearer. This would verify verses 8 to 9. I must admit to a difficulty I have in understanding the rightness of this portion in the KJV.

Chapter 14

This is the mechanism in action, and chapter 13, the oil that keeps this running smoothly.

Two other chapters as well as chapter 12 give us Christ's gifts to the assembly. Romans 12 – given by God and the individual is to feel his responsibility to nurture this gift. Ephesians 4:11 – given by an ascended Christ are given as foundational gifts. 1 Corinthians 12 – given by the Spirit for the up building and the edification of the saints. The emphasis in Corinthians is on the Spirit, in Ephesians on Christ. Note the repetition of the word *"body"*. *"For by one Spirit are we all baptized into one body"* (1 Cor. 12:13). *"The Spirit is like a thread that makes individual pearls into a necklace"* (G. Jones). 1 Cor. 12:27 – proper rendering *"Now ye are Christ's body."*

Chapter 15

This chapter is the resurrection chapter. There are two chapters in 1 Corinthians that stand apart and each is on one specific subject. The 13th chapter is all about divine love while chapter 15 contains much information about resurrection. Resurrection is the touchstone of Christianity. Without it, it would just be a philosophy built upon sand. If Christ had not risen from the dead what hope as humans would we have? "Eat, drink and be merry for tomorrow we die." But fellow Christian we can cry *"But now is Christ risen from the dead, and become the firstfruits of them that slept"* (v. 20).

This life, death and resurrection of Christ was *"not done in a corner"* (Acts 26:26). As our opening verses show, many witnessed the death, burial and resurrection of Christ.

The above subject takes up the first 23 verses of our chapter.

Verses 24 to 28 can be very confusing to some because of a lack of an antecedent to the pronoun. I will, with God's help, seek to put in the proper nouns. If any disagree with me or think otherwise, I would be glad to hear your thoughts.

"Then cometh the end (that is after the Great White Throne of judgment, (Rev. 20:7) *when He* (Christ) *shall have delivered up the kingdom to God* (the Father); *when He* (Christ) *shall have put down all rule and all authority and power. For He* (Christ) *must reign, till He* (God the Father) *hath put all enemies under His* (Christ's) *feet. The last enemy that shall be destroyed is death. For He* (God the Father) *hath put all things under His* (Christ's) *feet* (John 5:22). *But when He* (God the Father) *saith all things are put under Him* (Christ), *it is manifest that He* (God the Father) *is excepted, which did put all things under Him* (Christ). *And when all things shall be subdued unto Him* (Christ), *then shall the Son also Himself be subject unto Him* (God the Father) *that put all things under Him* (Christ), *that God* (the Trinity) *may be all in all."*

From verses 39 to 50 Paul contrasts the human body to the spiritual and also uses the symbol of a grain of wheat as to how it is sown as a bare grain and in order to bring forth new life it must be put in the ground and die. In this portion we read of the *"first man Adam"* and the *"last Adam"*; of the first man and the second. The second man is always the spiritual, e.g. "Esau and Jacob, Ishmael and Isaac, Cain and Abel," etc.

From verse 51 to the end of this chapter we are given important information as to the rapture of our bodies. They are so often referred to as "new bodies". But nowhere in Scripture do we read of "new" bodies. We shall have changed bodies. *"This mortal shall have put on immortality"* (1 Cor. 15:54). *"When He shall appear, we shall be like Him"* (1 John 3:2), that is morally. And He will change our bodies of humiliation (because they are subject to death), *"that it may be fashioned like unto His glorious body"* (Phil. 3:21). That is physically. "Like Jesus in that place of light and life supreme".

At the end spoken of in verse 24, when the thousand years of millennial peace have expired, then death and hell will be cast into the lake of fire (Rev. 20:14). There will be no more death. *"Death is swallowed up in victory"* (v. 54); Christ triumphed over death. At Calvary's cross Jesus annulled Satan's power over death and *"deliver them who through fear of death were all their lifetime subject to bondage"* (Heb. 2:15). *"Oh death, where is thy sting? O grave, where is thy victory? But thanks be to God, which giveth us the victory through our Lord Jesus Christ"* (1 Cor. 15:55). A Christian may fear dying but he is not afraid of death. Christ has taken the sting from death. Now death is but a servant to lead us into the presence of God.

Chapter 16

At various times in Paul's inspired epistles he touches on our giving, most particularly in 2 Corinthians chapters 8 and 9. We have the term *"the first day of the week"* (v. 2) which we see rarely in Scripture. The expression is found in each of the Gospels and once in Acts. It is the "new day" or the 8th day for the Christian. It is to be set apart.

The word *"communicate"* found in Galatians 6:6, Philippians 4:14, I Timothy 6:18 and Hebrews 13:16, has not only the thought of giving of yourself but also of giving of your substance, your money. The giving of what we have is a personal matter and Paul's instruction on that matter is discreet and wise. It should be as a man purposes in his own heart and is a matter between him and God. Do not make a vow as to giving unless you can fulfill it (Eccl. 5:4-5).

"Now if Timotheus come, see that he may be with you without fear: for he worketh the work of the Lord, as I also do. Let no man

therefore despise him" (v. 10). I have always felt that Paul feared that because of Timothy's timidness and youth that the saints would look down on him. Paul had the same word to Titus. I fear it is in our nature even as Christians to look down on our younger brothers. We should not do so, but encourage them and help to build them up.

As in the closing of other epistles by Paul he lists a number of his helpers: Apollos, Stephanas, Fortunatus, Achaicus, Aquila and Priscilla. All written, not only here, but in the Lamb's Book of Life. We are told to greet one another with a holy kiss. Custom and decorum would dictate our action. Phillips has "shake hands all around".

Paul closes with these solemn words *"If any man love not the Lord Jesus Christ, let him be Anathema Maranatha;"* accursed for Christ is coming. But Paul ends with *"The grace of our Lord Jesus Christ be with you"* and the writer gladly joins in this salutation.

Note: The author, being of the brethren persuasion, uses the word *"assembly"* when referring to *"ecclesia"*. The word *"church"* could be used as well. Indeed the Bible itself interchanges these two words (Heb. 12:23).

The word *"church"* is in the Greek *"Ecclesia"* and just means *"the called out ones"*. It is even used in reference to Israel (Acts 7:38).

THE *Second* EPISTLE OF PAUL THE APOSTLE TO THE *Corinthians*

Introduction

This letter is a follow up to the first and was written after the Corinthian assembly had heeded Paul's advice as to the man overtaken in his sin but also Paul's encouragement to the assembly to restore this same man who had repented and judged himself in this evil affair. As 1 Corinthians is like the first part of Isaiah, correction and judgment; 2 Corinthians is like the second part of Isaiah, comfort and consolation.

Chapter 1

God allows and sends trials in our lives for many reasons. One of them is that we might be empathetic with those who are passing through the same trials we have passed through. Remember that God is the God of all comfort or consolation. How sorely the church needs pastors and fathers. Those who can say the right word and also show through kind and thoughtful deeds their love and care for their brothers and sisters in Christ.

Who knew affliction as dear Paul and yet his fatherly care for God's people is evident in all his writings. We will never be of much help to God's people unless we love them much and are ready, like the Macedonians, to give of ourselves to others (ch. 8:5).

It cannot be overlooked that in this epistle Paul speaks much of himself and his labours for the Lord (verses 8-10). He was defending his apostleship against those who were criticizing his efforts.

Verse 14. This is one of the rare occasions in 1 or 2 Corinthians where Paul refers to the Day of the Lord Jesus. This would be the Rapture that he speaks of so much in Philippians (ch. 1:6, 10; 2:16).

Verses 19b-20. *"In Him was yea. For all the promises of God in Him are yea, and in Him Amen, unto the glory of God by us."* We might say that Christ's character is in opposition to the law for the essence of the law was, *"Thou shall not"*. Christianity is a positive faith. Christ's arms are opened wide and He bids all to come. There is no "NO" to be found in Him.

Chapter 2

Paul writes of his thoughts concerning his first letter to Corinth and how it caused him much pain to have to write it. He loved these saints but he felt his responsibility as God's servant so that he could not refrain from writing. But now upon the repentance of this failing one, Paul requests that they would bring him back into fellowship. *"Lest perhaps such a one should be swallowed up with overmuch sorrow"* (v. 7). We, as God's children, should never just cast the erring one out and then forget about him. Ezekiel 34 is a warning against this too oft practice. *"My sheep wandered… and none did search or seek after them"* (v. 6). God holds us responsible to go after the repentant sinner.

Chapter 3

Verse 1 speaks of a letter of commendation. How orderly and proper this is. Of course if the visitor is one who is familiar this is not necessary. Paul did not need such a letter to the Corinthians for these saints were his epistle written on his heart for he had fathered them in the faith.

Verse 6. *"Who also hath made us able ministers of the new testament; not of the letter, but of the spirit: for the letter killeth, but the Spirit giveth life."* How many of God's children have been turned aside by the cold legality of others who seek to replace the *"yea"* with the *"thou shall not"*. There is an expression that I have taken to my own heart, "God's love is ingenious, it goes beyond the letter of the law." Ruth was a Moabitess and according to the letter of the law, a Moabite was not to be accepted into fellowship with the Israelites until the tenth generation (Deut. 23:3). But love went beyond law and she was married to a *"mighty man of wealth"* (Ruth 2:1), named Boaz and she was accepted by the congregation of Israel. *"For thy daughter in law, which loveth thee, which is better to thee than seven sons, hath born him"* (Ruth 4:15).

Beloved saints of God let us keep this principle clearly in our mind when dealing with our beloved brethren. LOVE GOES BEYOND LAW! *"For the letter killeth, but the spirit giveth life"* (v. 6b).

Chapter 4

"Therefore seeing we have this ministry, as we have received mercy, we faint not." What ministry is Paul referring to? Why this ministry of grace versus law, of love overpowering legality, of all things being found positive in Christ and our Christian pathway. The next few verses are extremely precious (vv. 3 to 6). A natural man cannot fathom the things of God. The god of this world, Satan, has blurred men's eyes to the goodness of God and the work of Christ at Calvary. Satan is the god of this world religiously and the prince of this world politically. Do not expect any good emanating from this world for it is Satan's realm. I understand that in another translation verse 4 reads: *"They cannot see the light of the gospel of the glory of Christ, who is the image of God"* (NIV), that is, it is Christ who is glorious.

I recall how that many years ago on reading John 4:24 and John 1:18 I was greatly saddened that I would never behold God the Father. But then when I came to 2 Corinthians 4:4 and 6 my heart was lifted. Jesus could say to Philip *"he that hath seen Me hath seen the Father."* Beloved in that day when we look into the lovely face of Jesus we shall see the Father. Christ is the absolute essence of His Father both in image and likeness.

You may recall the story of Gideon in Judges 7:18-19. Gideon put a trumpet in every man's hand with empty pitchers and lamps within the pitchers. When Gideon blew the trumpet then all who were with him were also to blow their trumpets. And so when that tiny company came into the enemies' camp they blew the trumpets and broke the pitchers and the lamps within the pitchers shone forth.

What a marvellous illustration of this portion of 2 Corinthians. We are but earthen vessels, these vessels must be broken in order to let the light of Christ shine forth. In our chapter 4 verse 5 we read *"For we preach not ourselves, but Christ Jesus the Lord."* This is our trumpet. In verse 6 *"For God, who commanded the light to shine out of darkness, hath shined* (shone) *in our hearts."* Here is the candle, and then in verse 7 we have the vessel *"But we have this treasure in earthen vessels."* May we, beloved child of God, hide ourselves in Christ that the light of His love and wisdom might be trumpeted and shine forth to the whole world.

> I am an empty vessel scarce one thought,
> Or look of love to Thee I've ever brought;
> Yet I may come and come again, to Thee,
> With this the empty sinner's only plea,
> "Thou lovest me!"
>
> Hymn 72, Appendix, Little Flock

We have such a short period of time in this world. There are many short pithy verses in the Bible as to this. *"For we must needs die, and are as water spilt on the ground, which cannot be gathered up again"* (2 Sam. 14:14). Also *"For who knoweth what is good for man in this life, all the days of his vain life which he spendeth as a shadow"* (Eccl. 6:12). *"My days are swifter that a weaver's shuttle"* (Job 7:6). *"We spend our years as a tale that is told"* (Ps. 90:9). What are we doing with these short lives? Are we living them to glorify God our creator or to make things pleasant and comfortable for ourselves. In chapter 5:10 we read *"For we must all appear before the judgment seat of Christ,"* and in Exodus 23:15 we read *"And none shall appear before Me empty."* Dear fellow believers what will you have in that day to present to Christ? Paul could write in 2 Timothy 4:7 *"I have fought a good fight, I have finished my course, I have kept the faith."* Would to God that each one of us will be able to say that.

Verse 17. *"For our light affliction, which is but for a moment, worketh for us a far more exceeding and eternal weight of glory."* Well might we sing "It will be worth it all when we see Jesus".

Chapter 5

Paul continues in the same trend of thought as in the previous chapter. Our human bodies are often spoken of as tabernacles. But we have an eternal destiny with God. We desire with all our hearts to be *"absent from the body, and to be present with the Lord"* (v. 8).

Paul here is speaking of being clothed upon and unclothed (vv. 3-4). When we die our bodies are put in the grave but our spirits go to be with Christ in an unclothed state. We who die before the Rapture will be waiting to be clothed upon with our changed bodies that we read of in 1 Corinthians 15:49-54. The demons besought Jesus to let them go into the herd of swine for they could not tolerate an unclothed state (Matt. 8:31).

We have a blessed and a purifying hope, dear fellow Christian, and that is to hear the shout and to meet our Saviour in the air. We would much rather be *"absent from the body, and to be present with the Lord"* (v. 8).

How much confusion there has been surrounding verse 10. The secret word that unlocks any problem here is the "bema seat"; the seat upon which the judges sat to dispense rewards. It has nothing to do with our sins; that question was all settled at Calvary when Jesus cried *"It is finished"*. Paul often uses the simile of a runner to make his point. And what better word could be used for that seat before which all believers will appear as the reward seat. *"Know ye not that they which run in a race run all, but one receiveth the prize? So run, that ye may obtain"* (1 Cor. 9:24).

I might interject here the order in which these events will take place. First comes the Rapture when we shall receive changed bodies, morally and physically, like Christ, then the judgment seat of Christ will take place and then the marriage supper of the Lamb when Christ will receive His bride. *"His wife hath made herself ready"* (Rev. 19:7). I believe this refers to the bema seat of Christ where all our works will come up for review. The promised bride is made ready through the ceremony of the bema seat.

"Knowing therefore the terror of the Lord, we persuade men" (v. 11). There are a number of judgment seats: the judgment of the nations (Matt. 25:32); the bema seat (2 Cor. 5:10); and the Great White Throne of Judgment of those who are lost (Rev. 20:11). There will certainly be terror there. *"Behold, ye despisers, and wonder, and perish"* (Acts 13:41). I believe there are three time periods to be noted here. Today the unbeliever despises. When he stands before Christ at the Great White Throne of Judgment he will stand in awe and wonderment and the last words he will hear from Christ will be *"depart from me, all ye workers of iniquity"* (Luke 13:27), and perish.

This triune thought is also found in Luke 16:22-23. *"The rich man also died, and was buried; and in hell he lift up his eyes, being in torments"*.

I would ask my reader to deeply ponder the closing words of this chapter. How deep and profound they are, *"God was in Christ"*, Jesus as the perfect representative of His Father. *"Now then we are ambassadors for Christ, as though God did beseech you by us: we pray you in Christ's stead, be ye reconciled to God"* (vv. 19-20). What a blessed responsibility we have fellow Christian and what a glorious message we have to proclaim.

Verse 21. *"For He hath made Him* (Jesus) *to be sin for us, who knew no sin; that we might be made the righteousness of God in Him."* "What wondrous words are these. Their beauty who can tell."

Chapter 6

Paul writes graciously *"We then, as workers together"*. Then he gives us a list of those things that might befall a faithful child of God. I believe Paul is listing these trials that he himself had passed through. The words of verse 9 are engraved on John Nelson Darby's tombstone in Bournmouth England along with this short poem:

Lord let me wait for Thee alone,
My life be only this,
To serve Thee here on earth unknown
Then share Thy heavenly bliss.

Verses 11, 12 and 13 are exceedingly confusing in the way they are written in the King James Version. The NIV makes these verses much clearer. *"We have spoken freely to you, Corinthians, and opened wide our hearts to you. We are not withholding our affection from you, but you are withholding yours from us. As a fair exchange –I speak as to my children– open wide your hearts also."*

Verse 14. I have lived long enough to have seen broken hearts caused by not observing this verse. Mainly sisters in Christ marrying unsaved men whom they hope to convert after marriage. This rarely happens and the poor wife lives a wretched life of misery. This principle proclaimed here should be a rule in all facets of our lives. *"What concord hath Christ with Belial? or what part hath he that believeth with an infidel?"* (v. 15). We are told as in 1 Corinthians 3:16 that our bodies are the temple of the living God. What great sorrow this would keep our young people from if they would but observe and keep these words.

Chapter 7

Paul touches on some of the difficulties and trials he had passed through and on which he enlarges in chapters 11 and 12. He also writes concerning his first letter to the Corinthian assembly. He wrote that letter with a heavy heart and tears. But he was glad that he had sent it to them for it worked a great work in their hearts and consciences. Paul concludes *"In all things ye have approved yourselves to be clear in this matter"* (v. 11). That is in the matter of the brother who had committed adultery with his own stepmother.

Paul, in verses 14 and 16, speaks glowingly of the Corinthian saints. *"For if I have boasted any thing to him of you, I am not ashamed"* (v. 14), and *"I have confidence in you in all things."* (v. 16). He had told them in his first letter that they *"come behind in no gift"* (ch. 1:7).

Chapter 8

In the following two chapters Paul speaks of our giving to the Lord and our ministering to others. The word "communicate" as used in the New Testament does not only mean the giving of ourselves but of our substance (Gal. 6:6; Phil. 4:14; 1 Tim. 6:18; Heb. 13:16). The Macedonian saints had very little and I take it that Paul had argued against them giving him any financial help. But they insisted, but first proved their love for Paul by their giving of themselves to the work.

The Corinthian saints on the other hand were very wealthy, and Paul with well chosen words was working on their conscience to give abundantly as they had promised some time before but had not carried it out. Paul sends Titus and another unnamed brother to prepare the assembly at Corinth to have their promised monetary gift ready.

Chapter 9

Paul feared his boasting of the church at Corinth lest they not come through with their promised gift. Paul would feel ashamed of them if he came with his visiting brethren from Macedonia and they had not prepared the promised gift. Paul exhorts them to give *"every man according as he purposeth in his heart, so let him give; not grudgingly, or of necessity: for God loveth a cheerful giver"* (v. 7). In 1 Corinthians 16:2 Paul wrote *"Upon the first day of the week let every one of you lay by in store, as God hath prospered him."*

The important verse in these two chapters is found in chapter 8:9. *"For ye know the grace of our Lord Jesus Christ, that, though He was rich, yet for your sakes He became poor, that ye through His poverty might be rich."* This verse must humble our hearts when we think of that place that the Son had with His Father in eternity. He laid His glory by and came to earth to die that we might ever be beside Him through eternity. Beloved what a Saviour we have.

Second Corinthians

Chapter 10

In this chapter and the following one Paul takes his place as a fool that he might boast of his labours for Christ and His church. There were those who were attacking Paul on every hand, criticizing him about his labours for the Lord. He hints a number of times at his apparent physical problems *"who in presence am base among you"* (v. 1). *"For his letters, say they, are mighty and powerful; but his bodily presence is weak, and his speech contemptible"* (v. 10). *"But though I be rude in speech, yet not in knowledge"* (11:6). We can only guess to what Paul is referring. *"Do ye look on things after the outward appearance?"* (v. 7). Well if that was the case then Paul, as a fool, would boast of those things that he had passed through and done. Note the use of the word *"measure"* from verse 12 to 15. Paul would not boast of things that he had not done nor measure these things in comparison to other brethren. If we are to glory, then let us glory in the Lord (v. 17). *"But God forbid that I should glory, save in the cross of our Lord Jesus Christ"* (Gal. 6:14).

Chapter 11

Paul, being forced to boast as a fool lists some of those things he had suffered in his care of the church (verse 28).

"For I have espoused you to one husband, that I may present you as a chaste virgin to Christ" (v. 2). The Marriage Supper of the Lamb has not yet come (Rev. 19:7). The order of events I believe will be, first the Rapture, then the bema seat of Christ where all matters will be cleared up and rewards given. The wife has then as it were *"made herself ready"* (Rev. 19:7) and the marriage supper takes place.

From verse 5 to the end of the chapter Paul enumerates the various events and trials in his life. He did not wish to *"boast"* of these things but the weight of criticism pressed in upon him and as *"a fool"* (v. 16) he reminds the Corinthian saints of these things *"I am become a fool in glorying; ye have compelled me"* (Chapter 12:11).

After Paul has listed these sufferings the last item he mentions is *"Beside those things that are without, that which cometh upon me daily, the care of all the churches"* (v. 28). What servant of God ever took upon himself the care and concern of God's people as Paul did? He had a great love for all the saints but it appeared that the more he loved the less he was loved (ch. 12:15). If we are to be a help to God's people we must love them greatly. The English word "pastor" is derived from the word "pasture" where sheep graze and are at rest. The last words the Lord Jesus said to Peter were *"Shepherd my sheep"* and *"feed my sheep."* It has been my experience that those older brethren who have been of the greatest value in their declining years, spent much time in their early years in children and young peoples' work "feeding the lambs". Then later they were helping in shepherding by visiting widows and shut-ins and pasturing the flock. J.N. Darby said in his writings that the greatest need among God's people were pastors. I believe it is so today also. And finally *"Feed my sheep"*. When one has grown too old to travel or visit then he can be of invaluable help to feed the Lord's people from his storehouse of knowledge and wisdom from the Word of God.

Chapter 12

Paul continues in his comments on past experiences. The man in Christ of verse 2 is of course himself. Many believe that Paul had this vision when he was stoned and thought dead (Act 14:19). This was a miraculous experience and Paul heard things that he could not put into words, lest he should be exalted. Because of this experience he was given some kind of illness that physically caused him great pain. What this was we do not know. He cried to God to relieve him of the pain three times but the Lord's reply was *"My grace is sufficient for thee: for My strength is made perfect in weakness"* (v. 9). The proper translation of verse 7 is *"a thorn in the flesh to punch me"*. The words *"above measure"* should not be there because our flesh cannot be trusted to be exalted at all. (See NIV translation).

How could the Corinthian saints doubt Paul's authority as an apostle when mighty works were done among them *"in signs, and wonders, and mighty deeds"*(v. 12). They indeed were his epistles *"known and read of all men"* (2 Cor. 3:2).*"Behold, the third time I am ready to come to you"* (v. 14). We are not positive as to how many visits Paul made to Corinth but we can be assured it was at least three. In spite of all the effort that Paul expended to be a blessing to the Corinthians saints he would not seek to be financially aided by them (v. 13). He felt free to ask for help for other assemblies and saints but not for himself. Indeed he worked with his own hands as a tent maker to pay his way (1 Cor. 4:12; Acts 18:3). Paul mentions another brother without naming him (ch. 8:18, 22; 12:18). How many dear saints of God have their deeds but not their names mentioned in the Bible (1 Kings 13:1; 2 Kings 5:2). But God well knows their names for He has and is writing up His people (Ps. 87:6).

Chapter 13

Paul could speak and write as he does according to the power vested in him by Christ. He was a true apostle but one born out of due time, an abortive (1 Cor. 15:8). The Corinthian assembly had obeyed Paul in his request to put out from them this one who had sinned and he could boast of them to other assemblies but there was still need for correction. *"I write to them which heretofore have sinned, and to all other, that, if I come again, I will not spare"* (v. 2).

Satan felt his greatest victory was to see Christ on the cross but he was to learn that it was his greatest defeat *"that through death He might annul his power that had the power of death, that is, the devil"* (Heb. 2:14 NT). This man who claimed to be the King of Israel, had succumbed to the power of authority and was hanging on a cross of wood as a common thief. (John 18:33; 2 Cor. 13:4).

We are told a number of times to examine ourselves (1 Cor. 11:28; v. 5 of our chapter). This is a good and profitable exercise. *"I wisdom dwell with prudence, and find out knowledge which cometh with reflection or well considered thoughts"* (Prov. 8:12). That is from time to time we should review our pathway as one who at the end of the year reviews his accounts to see what he has done right and where he has made mistakes. *"Know ye not your own selves, how that Jesus Christ is in you, except ye be reprobates"* (v. 5). Paul himself did not wish to be a castaway (1 Cor. 9:27). This same word is found in Romans 1:28 and also means disqualified or rejected. It is not the same as an apostate. An apostate is one who was never real at all but took the place of being a believer (2 Pet. 2:20-22).

Paul had the same desire for God's people as Peter and John; that is their perfection, their full growth in Christ, that they might be presented faultless to God at His appearing. *"For so an entrance shall be ministered unto you abundantly into the everlasting kingdom of our Lord and Saviour Jesus Christ"* (2 Pet. 1:11). *"And now, little children, abide in Him; that, when He shall appear, we may have confidence, and not be ashamed before Him at His coming"* (1 John 2:28). *"For what is our hope, or joy, or crown of rejoicing? Are not even ye in the presence of our Lord Jesus Christ at His coming"* (1 Thess. 2:19)?

"Finally, brethren, farewell. Be perfect (full grown or mature), *be of good comfort, be of one mind, live in peace; and the God of love and peace shall be with you"* (v. 11). Here we have the God of love. In Philippians He is the *"God of peace"* (4:9), in 1 Peter 5:10 He is *"the God of all grace"*, and in 2 Corinthians 9:14 He is God of *"exceeding grace."*

Paul ends the epistle with an encouragement to show our love to one another. Philips' translation reads: "Shake hands all around". I suppose the society or environment in which we live determines this action. But the point is that we should not hide our love for one another *"Open rebuke is better than secret love"* (Prov. 27:5).

And now the whole Trinity is involved in Paul's closing words to the Corinthians. *"The grace of the Lord Jesus Christ, and the love of God, and the communion of the Holy Ghost, be with you all. Amen"* (13:14)

THE EPISTLE OF PAUL THE APOSTLE TO THE *Galatians*

The Galatian saints had many Jewish converts among them. They were perhaps superior to these Gentiles in the understanding of the Old Testament Scriptures and teachings. It must have been difficult for the Jews to give up their Jewish legalistic ceremonies, rules and laws but the danger was that they were reverting to these ways and striving to force these legal observances upon the Galatian Christians. Seeing the danger of this, Paul warns and exhorts them against this legalistic influence. In parts he writes strongly and in others he writes tenderly.

Paul no doubt had some physical infirmities. It is believed by some that he was a hunchback. From various Scriptures we know that he had that common ailment of eastern countries, eye trouble. In 2 Corinthians 10:10 they said of Paul that *"his bodily presence is weak, and his speech contemptible."* And in verse 1 of the same chapter, *"who in presence am base among you."* In 2 Corinthians 11:6, Paul says: *"but though I be rude in speech"*. The reference to his eyesight in chapter 4:15 must have touched the Galatian saints. *"That, if it had been possible, ye would have plucked out your own eyes, and have given them to me."* And in chapter 6:11 the better translation is, *"ye see how large a letter I have* (used) *written unto you."*

In most of Paul's epistles he used an amanuensis to dictate his letters to, but he writes the letter to the Galatians in his own hand. This was gracious of him because he had a cause against them and it would seem wiser to keep this between himself and the saints in Galatia.

The theme of the letter is the law versus grace. Paul even withstood Peter to his face over the matter because he was disenchanted by his conduct in acting one way when his fellow Jews were present and another when they were not (chapter 2:11-14).

We live by faith in Christ and Christ is our life (2:20; 3:11). We are dead to the law, for Christ nailed that to the cross, taking it out of the way. We are no longer under law but under grace. The law now has no power over us. Paul explains in chapter 3:17 *"that the covenant* (given to Abraham) *that was confirmed before of God in Christ, the law, which was four hundred and thirty years after, cannot disannul, that it should make the promise of none effect."* We are the children of promise and we are blessed with faithful Abraham. Abraham received the promise on the ground of faith. The law was given because of transgressions (3:19). Because of the Judaizing influence of some of these Jewish converts, the Galatians were slipping from grace and putting themselves once more under the law.

Paul reminds the Galatians that Christ had delivered them from the curse of the law, having been made a curse for them (3:13). The law had its place and was good as long as one was under a tutor or needed the controlling power of the law (i.e. an unsaved person). The law was used as a schoolmaster to bring them to Christ. It was not made for a righteous or born again man but for the lawless. Sin means lawlessness. (1 John 3:4, sin is lawlessness).

There were some in Galatia who had made themselves teachers of the law and they were troubling the saints by endeavouring to bring them under the law once again. Paul reminds them that a little leaven (evil doctrine, like yeast) leavens the whole lump (5:9).

He would wish that those who troubled the Galatian saints might be cut off (5:12).

After having sought, in the first four chapters, to bring them from under this evil teaching, Paul warns the Galatian saints about allowing the flesh to come in, using a quotation from the Jewish law to do so: *"For all the law is fulfilled in one word, even in this; Thou shalt love thy neighbour as thyself"* (5:14). If they would endeavour to gain righteousness by the keeping of the law, Paul points out that they would not be capable of keeping it, even in one point. It would be a very serious thing to put oneself under the law.

It would seem from chapter 5 that there was a display of the flesh going on in Galatia, which was bringing in wrath, strife, etc. Paul would classify their sins along with adultery, fornication, murder, etc.

Paul reminds them that the fruit of the Spirit is love, joy, peace etc. If we are Christ's, then these rather than the other would be seen in us, for we have crucified the flesh along with its lusts and we are to reckon the old man dead. Since we live in the Spirit, we should walk in the Spirit.

In chapter 6 Paul exhorts that those in Galatia who are not under these evil delusions of "law as opposed to grace" should seek to restore them in love but not, in doing so, get puffed up with the righteousness of their own position, for we are nothing in ourselves.

The word teaches us to help and provide practical support for those who teach. We should walk in love toward all men but especially to those who are likewise part of the household of faith.

We cannot glory in our knowledge or any spiritual gift that we may have but rather let our glorying simply be *"in the cross of our Lord Jesus Christ"* (6:14). *"And seekest thou great things for thyself? seek them not"* (Jer. 45:5).

THE EPISTLE OF PAUL THE APOSTLE TO THE *Ephesians*

Introduction

The book of Ephesians gives us the highest truths in the Bible for it takes us into the heavenlies. The key verse for Ephesians is found in verse 4 of chapter 1 *"chosen us in Him"*. We are seen seated with Christ in the heavenlies. We Christians are not being arrogant when we declare that we know God's will for it is His good pleasure to make it known to us (ch. 1;9). What a wonderful revelation that God is happy to make His will known to us His redeemed creatures. There are very few *"ifs"* in this book because of the certainty of the fulfillment of God's Word. Contrariwise there are many *"ifs"* in Hebrews because God is testing their faith. The writer of Hebrews warns the Hebrew saints of encroaching apostasy and letting slip the truths they have been taught (Heb. 2;1; 4:1; 6:4-6; 6:8; 10:26; 12:8). There is no such suggestion in Ephesians.

In the first three chapters our standing is given; in the following three, our state. The theme of unity runs throughout the whole epistle. Chapter 1: the unity of all things in Christ (v. 10). This verse has been declared, by some, to be the key to the Bible. Chapter 2: The unity of the Jew and Gentile (vv. 13-14), *"But now in Christ Jesus ye who sometimes were far off are made nigh by the blood of Christ. For He is our peace, who hath made both one, and hath broken down the middle wall of partition."* Chapter 3: The unity of the family of God, (vv. 14-15), *"For this cause I bow my knees unto the Father of our Lord Jesus Christ, of whom the whole family in heaven and earth is named."* Chapter 4: The epitome of unity (v. 3), the unity of the Spirit. There are seven *"ones"* and as we know, one is the number for unity and seven for divine completeness. One body, one Spirit, one hope, one Lord, one faith, one baptism and one God. Chapter 5 : The unity of the body of Christ with His church (vv. 25-32). Chapter 6 verses 1 to 10, the unity of the Christian home; verses 11 to 17 the unity of the Christian armour.

I would be remiss in not adding to this overview the seven glorious gifts that a resurrected Christ has given to each individual believer. This is not to be confused with the gifts given to the assembly which we read of in chapter 4.

Chapter 1

Verse 3. Our Father God has **blessed us** with all spiritual blessings in heavenly places in Christ.

Verse 4. God has **chosen us in Him** before the foundation of the world that we should be holy and without blame before Him in love.

Verse 5. Having **predestinated us** unto the adoption of children by Jesus Christ to Himself. And this was according to the good pleasure of His will.

Verse 6. We have been **accepted** by God **in the beloved.**

Verse 7. We have **redemption** through His blood, the forgiveness of sins.

Verse 11. In whom (Christ) also we have **obtained an inheritance.**

Verse 13. And we have been **sealed** with that Holy Spirit of promise.

Seven marvellous gifts; blessed chosen, predestinated, accepted, redeemed, obtained an inheritance and sealed with the Holy Spirit of promise. Notice the whole divine Trinity working on our behalf to bring us into the glorious liberty of the sons of God.

Besides these seven gifts God has made known unto us the mystery of His will (v. 9). And what is this revelation of His will but that in the fullness of time all His children will be gathered together in one. I count seven mysteries in the New Testament. Mysteries no more, for God has revealed the truth to us in His Word. *"Eye hath not seen, nor ear heard, neither have entered into the heart of man, the things which God hath prepared for them that love Him. But God hath revealed them unto us by His Spirit"* (1 Cor. 2:9-10). This quotation is taken from Isaiah 64:4, but the underlined words are not there for the Old Testament saints were kept in darkness as to those things. *"Jesus Christ, who hath abolished death, and hath brought life and immortality to light through the gospel"* (2 Tim. 1:10).

Is not this information awesome? We have had the mystery of God's will made known unto us and God hath revealed it to us, by His Spirit, the things which God hath prepared for us who love Him. *"What shall we then say to these things?"* (Rom. 8:31).

Verse 12. There are many ways we can glorify God. Our lives should be lived to the praise of His glory. Indeed we were created to glorify God. *"For I have created him for My glory, I have formed him; yea, I have made him"* (Isa. 43:7). When we open our lips in praise to God we glorify Him. (1 Pet. 4:14; Ps. 50:23).

Verse 13. Being sealed is, and has been, an arguable point. In the days when letters were sealed with hot wax and the senders' symbol was stamped upon it the message therein was safe and complete. We, Christians, have been sealed with that Holy Spirit of promise. We are safe and secure.

Verse 14. Our earnest is a token of things to come. It is a pledge that the work begun will be completed. The Holy Spirit has been sent as a comforter and a pledge.

Chapter 2

The theme of this entire chapter is the fact that the Gentile has been brought into the same relationship with Christ as the Jew. God has given each of us believers a gift and this gift is faith (v. 8). It is not through our works we are saved, but through the gift of faith alone. *"Not by works of righteousness which we have done, but according to His mercy He saved us"* (Tit. 3:5).

I love the two *"buts"* in this chapter. *"But God, who is rich in mercy, for His great love wherewith He loved us… hath quickened us together with Christ, (by grace ye are saved)"* (vv. 4-5). And *"But* now in Christ Jesus ye (we Gentiles) *who sometimes were far off are made nigh by the blood of Christ"* (v. 13). *"And, having made peace through the blood of His cross, by Him to reconcile all things unto Himself "* (Col. 1:20).

If we search hard enough we will find little nuggets scattered throughout the Scriptures. Ephesians chapter 2:10 is a case in point. The Greek says that we are His *"poema created in Christ Jesus unto good works."* Is this not beautiful? We are God's poems seen and read by all men. This word is only found in one other place: Romans 1:20

Verse 15. Through the death of Christ He has made in Himself of two (Jew and Gentile) one new man. He has broken down the wall of partition between us. *"He has reconciled both unto God in one body"* (v. 16) and preached peace to us Gentiles so that we are no longer considered *"strangers and foreigners, but fellow citizens with the saints, and of the household of God"*(v. 19). The house contains the household.

"Remember, that ye being in time past Gentiles in the flesh…that at that time ye were without Christ, being aliens from the commonwealth of Israel, and strangers from the covenants of promise, having no hope, and without God in the world. But now in Christ Jesus ye (Gentiles) *who sometimes were far off are made nigh by the blood of Christ"* (2:11-13). *"Henceforth walk not as other Gentiles walk, in the vanity of their mind"* (4:17).

Chapter 3

There are four epistles Paul wrote while he was a prisoner in Rome, but he never speaks of this, but rather as a prisoner or bond slave of Jesus Christ.

It is of extreme importance to understand that Paul was given a special portion of the gospel which he speaks of here and in Colossians chapter 1:24-27. The words in Colossians, chapter 1:24 *"fill up"* is exactly the same word used in verse 25 *"to fulfill (fill up) the word of God."* God gave this ministry to Paul to complete the gospel. It was a mystery *"which hath been hid from ages and from generations, but now is made manifest to His saints"* (v. 26). And what is the revelation of this wondrous news: that *"God would* *make known what is the riches of the glory of this mystery among the Gentiles; which is **Christ in you, the hope of glory**"* (Col. 1:27). Or as Ephesians 3:6 puts it *"that the Gentiles should be fellowheirs, and of the same body, and partakers of his promise in Christ by the gospel."*

Paul was particularly elected by Christ to go to the Gentiles with this good news (Rom. 11:13). The rejection of Christ by the Jewish nation resulted in the turning of God to the Gentiles and Paul was raised up for this very purpose (Act 28:28).

This was almost unbelievable news to the Jews. Indeed God in a special way, and by means of a vision, had to reveal to Peter that the Gentiles also were to be included among God's chosen people and that indeed salvation had also come to the Gentiles (Acts 10:9-16; Rom. 11:11).

In verse 8 we have one of God's superlatives. A superlative is when we cannot find words to describe what certain information means to us. *"Unto me... is this grace given, that I should preach among the Gentiles the **unsearchable** riches of Christ."* Other superlatives are: Ephesians 3:19 *"The love of Christ, which **passeth knowledge**"*; Romans 11:33 *"How **unsearchable** are His judgments, and His ways past finding out"*; I Peter 1:8 *"Whom having not seen, ye love; in whom though now ye see Him not, yet believing, ye rejoice with **joy unspeakable** and full of glory"*; 2 Corinthians 9:15 *"Thanks be unto God for His **unspeakable gift**"*; and Philippians 4:7 *"The peace of God, which passeth **all understanding**."* Verses 14-15 brings before us the unity of the family in our Father God. In one sense God is the Father of all creation (ch. 4:6 and Isa. 9:6 *"The Father of the everlasting;"* proper rendering). Israel could speak of God as their Father nationally (Isa. 64:8) but we Christians know God as our Father in a very personal way. Jesus taught His disciples to pray *"Our Father which art in heaven"* (Matt. 6:9). One of Christ's specific purposes in coming into the world was to make God, His Father, known to us (Matt. 11:27).

Chapter 4

This chapter contains the epitome of unity. There are seven *"ones"* from verses 4 to 6. In verse 4 we have a small circle; the church, the one body of Christ. In verse 5 we have a widening circle which takes in Christendom and in verse 6 an ever widening circle which takes in all creation.

In Psalm 68:18 Christ receives gifts for men but in Ephesians 4:8 those gifts are dispersed to man. The gifts to the assemblies are listed three times in the New Testament: 1 Corinthians 12:8 -11; Romans 12:6-8; and Ephesians 4:11-12. In each one a different person of the Trinity is the donor of these gifts. Here in Ephesians chapter 4, these gifts are given by an ascended Christ. Christ is prominent in Ephesians but the Spirit in Corinthians. And so the gifts in chapter 12 of 1 Corinthians are given by the Spirit; in Romans 12 it is *"As God hath dealt to every man"* (v. 3). Thus the whole of the Trinity is involved in the disbursement of these gifts to the church.

There is an enigma suggested in verse 9: *"Now that He ascended, what is it but that He also descended first into the lower parts of the earth?"* These lower parts of the earth are alluded to several times in the Bible but never explained (Ps. 63:9; Isa. 44:23; Ps. 139:15). Would it be speaking of the unseen world, the place of departed spirits, Hades, Sheol? In Psalm 16:10 Christ prophetically says *"thou wilt not leave my soul in Sheol."* And in I Samuel 28:19 the prophet Samuel is brought up from Sheol. Samuel tells Saul that *"tomorrow shalt thou and thy sons be with me."* There is much that we do not understand. *"The secret things belong unto the Lord our God"* (Deut. 29:29).

Verse 16. I continually marvel at the compactness of the words in this verse. How amazing it is in its terseness yet completeness. Could the thoughts contained therein be put any better? The student of English grammar and construction could do no better than study the Word of God. The knowledge of the Bible can be seen in much of Shakespeare's writings. Even the cadence that he uses at times is copied from Scripture. e.g. "This above all: to thine own self be true" (Hamlet). *"Take heed unto thyself, and unto the doctrine"* (1 Tim. 4:16).

The thought of unity which unites the entire epistle is continued in three verses in this 4th chapter: Verse 3, the unity of the Spirit; verse 13, the unity of faith and verse 16, the unity of the body of Christ.

Verse 21 contains a monumental statement *"Ye have heard Him and have been taught by Him, as the TRUTH IS IN JESUS"*. The verse is akin to Revelation 19:10 *"The testimony of Jesus is the spirit of prophecy"*. Also *"Where the Spirit of the Lord is, there is liberty. But we all, with open face beholding as in a glass the glory of the Lord, are changed into the same image from glory to glory, even as by the Spirit of the Lord"* (2 Cor. 3:17-18). (marginal reading: "of the Lord the Spirit").

In Ephesians chapter 4 and Colossians 3 (vv. 8, 10, 12, 14) we are told to put on and put off. We Christians have been made new creatures in Christ and the old man has been crucified with Him. *"I am crucified with Christ: nevertheless I live; yet not I, but Christ liveth in me: and the life which I now live in the flesh I live by the faith of the Son of God, who loved me, and gave Himself for me"* (Gal. 2:20). Oh that we would surrender ourselves to the instruction here; how Christ- like we would be.

Chapter 5

How often in the Epistles the doctrine is given in the first part and then the practical carrying out of the doctrine in the final part.

Verses 1 to 13 – Immorality in all its filthy characteristics permeates our whole western society. Enoch, warned us of this ungodliness which would be rampant in a coming day (Jude 14-15). We are living in that day just before the Lord's coming for His saints. Our young people have lasciviousness rammed into their minds wherever they turn. It is up to parents to seek to safeguard their children from such uncleanness. Example is one of the best deterrents. It is so important that we adults shine forth as lights for Christ, especially in our homes and in our interrelationships with our children. It is so true that as the twig is bent, so the tree shall grow. *"Be not overcome of evil, but overcome evil with good"* (Rom. 12:21). In Isaiah we read in reference to Jesus *"Behold, a virgin shall conceive, and bear a son, and shall call His name Emmanuel. Butter and honey shall He eat, that He may know to refuse the evil, and choose the good"* (ch. 7:14-15). Let us occupy our minds and hearts with only that which is good, as we read in Philippians 4:8,*"Think on these things"*.

Verse 14 *"Awake thou that sleepest, and arise from the dead, and Christ shall give thee light."* These words are speaking to an unsaved soul for it says *"Arise from the dead."* But in Romans 13:11 similar words are used to a believer. It is possible to get so far from the Lord and the Christian pathway that it appears that we are as the dead in Ephesians 5:14. We are told to *"shine (for the Lord) as lights in the world; holding forth the word of life"* (Phil. 2:15-16). How sad when we cannot tell a believer from those of this world.

The word of God uses the simile of marriage for the relationship of Christ and His bride, the church. It was so also with Jehovah and Israel in the Old Testament. But because of Israel's whoredom (idolatry) Jehovah was forced to divorce her (Isa. 50:1). This could never be the case with Christ and the church. We believers are inseparably joined to Christ for He purchased us with His own blood. The bride of Christ is a present from God to His Son. But then we read in verse 28 *"So ought men to love their wives as their own bodies."* This wonderful example of Christ and the church is put forth as a model to husbands. In counseling married couples I have asked the husband how often he tells his wife how much he loves and appreciates her. There is almost always a hushed silence. This lack of affection is often at the root of marital difficulties. *"Let every one of you in particular so love his wife even as himself; and the wife see that she reverence her husband"* (v. 33).

Chapter 6

In this chapter the theme of unity continues threefold; the unity of the Christian home, (vv. 1 to 4); the unity of the Christian life (vv. 5 to 9); and the unity of the Christian armour (vv. 11 to 17). Notice there is no armour for the back parts for we should never turn our backs on Satan but rather resist him (Jas. 4:7). And beloved brethren we need to put on the **whole** armour for we need each piece. *"For we wrestle not against flesh and blood, but against principalities, against powers, against the* *rulers of the darkness of this world, against spiritual wickedness in high places"* (v. 12).

"Praying always" (v. 18). That is to be continuously in the attitudes of prayer and dependence upon God. To walk with Christ in the attitude of prayer each day is one of the sweetest experiences that one can have. *"Rejoice evermore. Pray without ceasing. In everything give thanks: for this is the will of God in Christ Jesus concerning you"* (1 Thess. 5:16-18).

May the Lord of all wisdom bless these thoughts to our hearts and minds.

THE EPISTLE OF PAUL THE APOSTLE TO THE *Philippians*

Introduction

This epistle is another of Paul's prison epistles written and delivered to the Philippians by Epaphroditus from Rome. The epistle is different in theme from Ephesians and Colossians. Its theme is of our common Christian experiences, of the normal pattern for the Christian life. As a Christian we have a new life in Christ and are to consider the old man dead unto sin. The word sin is never mentioned in Philippians. The words *"joy"* and *"rejoicing"* are found 16 times in the epistle, for this should be the main characteristics of the new man. Another theme is the oneness and unity of the Christian body. We find the words *"you all"* and *"us"* many times as well as the word *"same"*. We are seen as one in the eyes of God in Philippians. In chapter 1 the gospel is mentioned five times: verse 5, the fellowship of the gospel, verse 7, the defense and confirmation of the gospel, verse 12, the furtherance of the gospel, verse 17, again the defense of the gospel, and finally verse 27, the faith of the gospel.

Chapters Themes

In Chapter 1, Christ is our **life** or **purpose**; in chapter 2, Christ is seen as our **pattern**; in chapter 3, He is seen as our **object** or **prize** and in chapter 4, He is seen as our **strength** or **power**. To make these easy to remember, Christ is our **purpose, our pattern, our prize and our power**.

Read over these chapters carefully keeping these four "P's" in mind. Here is a very important fact of which to get hold. When we believe in the person of Christ we are saved but when we believe His Word we are sealed. (Kelly, Ephesians p. 38; Acts p. 165). *"In whom also after ye believed, ye were sealed"* (Eph. 1:13).

The day of Jesus Christ is found almost exclusively in this epistle (ch. 1:6, 10; ch. 2:16). There are 4 days spoken of in the New Testament:

1. man's day, when man's will and power bears rule. *"This is your hour and the power of darkness"* (Luke 22:53).

2. the day of Christ we find exclusively in Philippians; the day when Christ will come to take His own to glory.

3. the day of the Lord which will last from the Rapture of the church until the beginning of the fourth day; the day of God.

4. And the day of God which will be the eternal state (2 Pet. 3:12).

Another theme repeated is the word *"mind"*. In chapter 1:17, we are to have the **gospel mind**; in chapter 2:2 we are told to be **like minded** and to **be of one mind**; in verse 5 of the same chapter we are to have a **humble mind**; in chapter 3:16, we are to **mind the same thing**; to have unity of mind and in verse 19 we are told of those who mind earthly things. Then again in chapter 4:2, two troublesome sisters were told to **have the same mind**.

The other word so common in Philippians is *"same"*. Chapter 1:30, the **same conflict**; chapter 2:2, the **same love**; in chapter 3:16 we have the **same rule**, the **same cause** and the **same thing**. So you see, the most used expressions, *"You all, us, mind* and *same,"* would all urge the saints at Philippi to go on together in unity in the things of Christ. God hates disunity and those who sow it (Prov. 6:19).

Chapter 3

In verse 2 we are warned to beware of dogs (see Gal. 5:15): those who creep in among God's people and bring discord and division. Also we are warned of the concision; that is those who are mutilators of the flesh. These would be the ones who bring in the religious flesh among God's people, observing days and rituals; telling God's people to live under rules and regulations. This **is not** normal Christianity, for Christ has set us free from all the legalism and ritualism of the law. We are told in verse 3 that we are to have no confidence in the (religious) flesh, but to worship God in the Spirit and rejoice in Christ Jesus. The whole triune God is mentioned here.

In verse 5 Paul speaks of seven prides that he and all of us succumb to: ceremonial pride, national pride, family pride, positional pride, religious or ecclesiastical pride, legalistic pride and pride in our works. But Paul having practiced these things, until he met Christ on the road to Damascus, now counted them all but refuse *"for the excellency of the knowledge of Christ Jesus my Lord: for whom I have suffered the loss of ALL THINGS, and do count them but refuse, that I may win Christ"* (v. 8).

One of the most beautiful acknowledgements that Paul makes anywhere in his writings is found in verses 9 and 10 of chapter 3: *"And be found in Him, not having mine own righteousness, which is of the law, but that which is through the faith of Christ, the righteousness which is of God by faith: THAT I MAY KNOW HIM, and the power of His resurrection, and the fellowship of His sufferings, being made conformable unto His death."* Would to God, dear fellow believer, that we all had that same desire.

I wish to make one verse in chapter 3:15 clear, as it is somewhat obtuse in the KJV. In the NIV it reads: *"and if on some point you think differently, that too will God make clear to you."* How much division and sorrow this word would save us from if we would but heed it. In chapter 3:21, we should not have the word *"vile"*. God creates nothing vile. It should read *"bodies of humiliation"* because we are subject to death; Christ was not (Acts 2:24). *"No man taketh it from Me, but I lay it down of Myself"* (John 10:18).

Chapter 4

In this chapter two sisters were not getting along. The least dissension in the assembly brings in sorrow and trouble. Sheep will not drink if the waters are disturbed. Verse 5 should read *"let your moderation be known unto all men. The Lord is* **close by (or watching)**.*"*

Although Paul had been in prison for four years up to this point, he could say *"rejoice in the Lord alway: and again I say rejoice"* (v. 4). Could you or I do the same in such a situation?

Devotedness is to give oneself up wholly for an object; supplication is intensified prayer (v. 6).

In verse 7, we have one of God's many superlatives: *"and the peace of God, which passeth all understanding"*. Other examples in Scripture are: *"How unsearchable are His judgments, and His ways past finding out"* (Rom. 11:33); *"And to know the love of Christ, which passeth knowledge"* (Eph. 3:19); *"the unsearchable riches of Christ"* (Eph. 3:8); *"ye rejoice with joy unspeakable"* (1 Pet. 1:8). Peace which passeth all understanding, ways unsearchable, the love of Christ which passeth knowledge, and the unsearchable riches and joy unspeakable of Christ: five superlatives.

Finally we are encouraged in verses 4 to 8 to set our minds and hearts on things above. *"Think on these things."*

How touching are these words from the prisoner of Rome but yet the bond slave through love of Jesus Christ. Even in these circumstances Paul could say: *"But I HAVE ALL, and abound"* (v. 18). Paul's example to all who knew him was a witness even unto Caesar's household. A coming day will declare the fruits of Paul's joy in Christ before all, even those of Caesar's household while in bonds (v. 22). Who were these souls thus brought to Christ through Paul's joy in Christ though in chains and in prison? We shall know one day.

Conclusion

Having given the four "P's" of each chapter, the following are the verses that illustrate this. Chapter 1, **Purpose;** verse 21, *"for to me to live is Christ"*; chapter 2, **Pattern;** verse 5, *"let this mind be in you, which was also in Christ Jesus"*; chapter 3, **Prize;** verse 10, *"that I may know Him, and the power of His resurrection,* *and the fellowship of His sufferings, being made conformable unto His death;"* and chapter 4, **Power;** verse 13, *"I can do all things through Christ which strengtheneth me."* We receive power in our Christian life by setting our own minds on things above, (vv. 8-9) and living them out in our lives.

THE EPISTLE OF PAUL THE APOSTLE TO THE *Colossians*

Introduction

The key to Colossians is found in verse 27 of chapter 1. *"...Christ in you, the hope of glory."* In Ephesians we are seen in Christ seated with Him in the heavenlies. In Colossians, Christ is to be seen in His children who are here to represent Christ in His likeness to the world while He is in the glory. To illustrate this I might say that you look much like your father. That you represent him in your little idiosyncrasies, the way you walk, or the way you look. But your unique mannerism, cause me to remark : "why you are the very image of your father."

While Christ was in the world He was the light of the world but now that He has returned to His Father we are to be the light of the world (Matt. 5:14). Likeness is representative (1 Cor. 15:49), but image is moral (1 John 3:2). *"And God said, let us make man in our image, and after our likeness"* (Gen. 1:26). Christ is the very image and likeness of the invisible God (1:15).

Paul had never been to Colosse (1:2), but he had heard of their faith and of the love they had to all the saints (1:4). Note the use of the word *"all"* in Colossians.

Many verses have to do with our walk in this world for we are ambassadors for Christ (2 Cor. 5:20). In chapter 1 we have *"all the saints"*, *"all the world"*, *"all pleasing"*, *"all right"* and *"all things."* Our walk should encompass all these things in our lives.

Chapter 1

In verses 25 to 27 Paul was given a distinct portion of the gospel by a risen Christ to fulfil or complete the Word of God. This mystery was hid for ages and there is no suggestion of it in the Old Testament Paul would now make manifest this mystery among the Gentiles which is *"Christ in you, the hope of glory."* (See also Eph. 3:3).

Christ is *"the image of the invisible God"* (1:15). *"And by Him all things consist"*(are held in place) (1:17). *"In whom are hid all the treasures of wisdom and knowledge"* (2:3). *For in Him dwelleth all the fulness of the Godhead bodily"* (2:9). And He *"is our life"* (3:4).

Chapter 2

In this chapter Paul warns the saints at Collose of rationalism and philosophy; the former reasons and the latter questions (vv. 4-8). *"For in Him dwells all the fulness of the Godhead"* (Theotes, God in the absolute sense). This is the only time this word is used in Scripture.

In verses 16 to the end Paul again warns them of those who would bring in philosophy, vain deceit and ritualism.

Chapter 3

In chapter 3 we are directed to seek those things which are above. In verse 2 it should read *"Set your **hearts** on things above,"* for Christ is our life. We are to daily put to death (mortify) our bodies to the sinful things of the flesh (vv. 5-9). We are told what to *"put off"* and what to *"put on "*(vv. 8, 10). In verses 12-13 there are seven things we are to put on. Love binds all these things to us (v. 14). *"Let the word of Christ dwell in you richly"* (v. 16).

In Colossians as in other epistles Paul puts the doctrine before the saints and then the practical carrying out of this doctrine (3:18 to 4:1).

Chapter 4

In the final portion of the 4th chapter Paul lists those who were with him in Rome and who ministered unto him while he was imprisoned there. Tychicus and Onesimus, Philemon's runaway slave, wrote and carried this letter to the saints at Colosse. Paul speaks of Onesimus as *"a faithful and beloved brother, who is one of you"* (v. 9). Was Onesimus returning to his master Philemon on this trip? Aristarchus who was imprisoned with Paul and Marcus, Barnabas' nephew is mentioned next. I have always felt it gracious that Marcus is not left in limbo as in Acts 15:37 to 40. Paul writes *"if he come unto you, receive him"* (v. 10). In 2 Timothy 4:11 *"He is profitable to me for the ministry"*. It is the same with Hezekiah's wicked son Manasseh. The last word concerning him in 2 Kings is *"And Manasseh seduced them* (Judah) *to do more evil than did the nations whom the Lord destroyed before the children of Israel"* (2 Kgs. 21:9). But the Word of God doesn't leave him there for we read in 2 Chronicles that while he was imprisoned by the Assyrians he prayed to God and *"he besought the Lord his God, and humbled himself greatly before the God of his fathers, and prayed unto Him: and He was entreated of him and heard his supplications... Then Manasseh knew that the Lord He was God"* (2 Chron. 33:12-13). How gracious of God not to leave these men in their sad conditions in the world. There are other similar cases in the Scriptures.

Then we have Jesus who was called Justus. I have always felt that Justus felt he was unworthy to bear that blessed name his parents had given him so he insisted on being called "Justus".

"Epaphras, who is one of you, a servant of Christ... always labouring fervently for you in prayers, that ye may stand perfect and complete in all the will of God." (v. 12). How precious and how perfect was this servant of God to have God's children ever before him. In chapter 1:7 of our present epistle we have further characteristics of Epaphras recorded. What is being recorded in God's book about you and me? (Ps. 87:6; Mal. 3:16).

What can we say about this beloved, humble physician Luke? Earlier he hid himself in the book of the Acts which he wrote. He tells us nothing of his hardships and what he had to endure in his journeys with Paul. His name is on God's honour role for all eternity.

Paul has little to say about Demas. Did he see the seeds of departure growing in Demas' heart at this time? The world had a greater attraction for Demas than being a lowly servant of Christ (2 Tim. 4:10).

It is rather interesting to read of these epistles that Paul wrote at the same time. One to Colosse and one to Laodicea.

The one was inspired and forms part of our New Testament, while the other, I am sure, was profitable, but was not inspired. Paul must have written hundreds of letters but the Spirit of God has chosen only those which were inspired by Him.

Finally in verse 17 we have these important words *"Say to Archippus, take heed to the ministry which thou hast received in the Lord, that thou fulfil it"*. How many servants of God to whom He has given the gift of teaching, pastoring or preaching have not fulfilled it because of various reasons: work, family, wealth, the fear of man, etc. God does not give a gift unless He intends it to be used. If any such young or old, male or female, read these remarks I would earnestly encourage you to put this God given gift first in your life.

Conclusion

The summation of all that Paul is seeking to bring before the saints in Collose is found in chapter 4:5. *"Walk in wisdom toward them that are without."* We are here in this world to glorify Christ (Isa. 43:7) and to be His representatives as a light to this darkened world.

THE *First* EPISTLE OF PAUL THE APOSTLE TO THE *Thessalonians*

Introduction

1st Thessalonians could well be the first inspired epistle to the assemblies or individuals that Paul ever wrote. It is not my purpose in these short overviews to revue the historicity or background to them. I only wish to bring out the spiritual truth behind the words in a cursory way as the Spirit of God leads. Neither do I wish to parrot the thoughts of other expositors on the same subject. But in a prayerful attitude bring fresh thoughts to the young.

The truth of God's Word never changes from generation to generation but the circumstances of life and society as a whole do. The Israelites were not to eat stale manna but to pick it fresh every day (Ex. 16:21). Apart from this, even language becomes antiquated, so that the young of today have great difficulty to interpret the language of the past. The Spirit of God never stops supplying the truth in its freshness and I thank God that each generation produces expositions of the Scriptures that suit the day in which we live (Acts 13:36).

The church at Thessalonica was a young church. The members were babes in Christ. They had been called out (*ecclesia*) of darkness into light; they had turned to God from idols (1:9). Paul writes to them in a tender loving way (2:7) as a father to his children (2:11). He had heard of their *"work of faith, and labour of love, and patience of hope in our Lord Jesus Christ"* (1:3).

To give a very brief theme of First and Second Thessalonians: Paul in the 1st epistle sets out to establish the truth in their hearts as to the Lord's coming (4:14-18). We call this the Rapture (snatching away) though this word is not actually found in the Bible. Each chapter ends with either the Rapture or the appearing.

2nd Thessalonians is written to refute a lie. That is, that the day of the Lord had already happened (2 Thess. 2:2). The worst mistranslation in the King James version is this very verse and why its obvious mistake has never been corrected I do not understand. To leave it as the "day of Christ" would confound the whole truth about each of these days. The "day of Christ" is when Christ comes to claim His bride as in 1st Thessalonians ch. 4:16. It will be a day of great joy for believers when we are caught away to be eternally with Christ. The Epistle to the Philippians says much about the "day of Christ". The "day of the Lord", on the other hand, will be a day of darkness, bloodshed and horror like the world has never seen and will begin right after the rapture of the church. The book of Joel describes it. These then are the two basic themes and what is written in each of these two epistles revolves around them.

Let us then look at these chapters in a more detailed way.

Chapter 1

As pointed out earlier, these dear saints were but babes in Christ. Paul's words are tenderly and affectionately written to them. The salutation is the same as in all his previous letters, *"grace be unto you and peace"* (v. 1). This does not change until 2nd Timothy, where *"mercy"* is introduced along with *"grace and peace"* (v. 2). Though babes in Christ, their faithfulness had made them an example to the other assemblies (1:7). And, though young in faith, they anticipated the Lord's return for them, *"which delivered us from the wrath to come"* (1:10).

Chapter 2

Paul writes of his introduction to the church at Thessalonica and how that there was much fruit produced at that time. He came to them in sincerity and truth and was gentle as a nurse among them (v. 7) and as a father dealing with his children (v. 11). He writes in loving, affectionate terms. God had prepared their hearts to receive His word (v. 13).

Paul had the heart of a true pastor. *"For what is our hope, or joy, or crown of rejoicing? Are not even ye in the presence of our Lord Jesus Christ at His coming?"* (v. 19, the Rapture). Peter also had the same fatherly care and concern for those he ministered to. *"Wherefore the rather, brethren, give diligence to make your calling and election sure: for if ye do these things, ye shall never fall: for so an entrance shall be ministered unto you abundantly into the everlasting kingdom of our Lord and Saviour Jesus Christ"* (2 Pet. 1:10,11). Or as another has said, Peter desired that his brethren would enter the harbour of heaven with all flags flying. John also was like minded. *"And now, little children, abide in Him; that, when He shall appear, we may have confidence, and not be ashamed before Him at His coming"* (1 John 2:28, the Rapture). We will never serve God's people well unless we love them well and desire their ultimate blessing.

Chapter 3

As we read through 1st Thessalonians we do not find one word of reproach, as we do in almost all the other of Paul's letters. Chapter 3 is one continuous expression of affection and exposes Paul's love and longing to see, once again, these dear saints of God. He had sent Timothy, his son in the faith, before him that he might know of their welfare. Timothy returned to Paul with a report of their faith and charity. Paul was comforted by this report. With what love Paul speaks to them in verse 10 of his prayers for them and his earnest desire to see them once again. *"Night and day praying exceedingly that we might see your face, and might perfect that which is lacking in your faith."* At the end of the chapter, verse 13, Paul refers to the appearing, when Christ shall return with His saints, as in chapter 4:14, *"even so them also which sleep in Jesus will God bring with Him".* We must not confuse the appearing (ch. 4:14; Rev. 19:14) with the Rapture (4:16-17). At the Rapture Christ comes for His saints, at the appearing Christ comes with His saints.

Chapter 4

Paul seeks to give guidance on a matter that he has spoken of in other epistles, e.g.- 1st Corinthians chapters 6 and 7. In

Romans 12:1 we read, *"I beseech you therefore, brethren, by the mercies of God, that ye present your bodies a living sacrifice, holy, acceptable unto God, which is your reasonable* (intelligent) *service"*. And in 1st Corinthians 6:13, 18 *"the body is not for fornication, but for the Lord; and the Lord for the body...flee fornication...he that committeth fornication sinneth against his own body."* And again in our epistle, chapter 5:23, *"and the very God of peace sanctify you* (set you apart) *wholly; and I pray God your whole **spirit** and **soul** and **body** be preserved blameless unto the coming of our Lord Jesus Christ"* (the Rapture).

These verses speak for themselves and do not need clarification. Remember, though, that *"marriage is honourable in all, and the bed undefiled"* (Heb. 13:4). God would have us not only to live pure lives but have pure thoughts.

The latter part of the chapter is taken up with the return of the Lord for His people (vv. 13-17). Those who sleep in Jesus (the dead) will at the shout rise first, including the Old Testament saints, from Adam on. And then we who are alive on this earth shall be gathered together with them on the cloud to meet the Lord in the air : *"so shall we ever be with the Lord"*(v. 17). Blessed truth. This passage and the one in 1st Corinthians chapter 15 are the clearest, in all of God's Word, as to the Rapture.

Chapter 5

This chapter speaks mostly of *"the day of the Lord"* (v. 2). This day or time will be a day of darkness and not light. *"A day of darkness and of gloominess, a day of clouds and of thick darkness"* (Joel 2:2). I know of no portion of Scripture other than Joel where the "day of the Lord" is so clearly explained. The expression *"the times and seasons"* (Dan. 2:21) would include this period, which will begin right after the Rapture and go on until the beginning of the eternal state. *"The day of God"* (the eternal state), when righteousness will dwell upon the earth (2 Pet. 3:12-13), will begin immediately following the millennium.

It is never said concerning the church that the Lord will come as *"a thief in the night"* (v. 2). That is always associated with the Lord's appearing; His coming in power and glory to judge the earth (Matt. 24:30). *"They that sleep, sleep in the night"* (v. 7). We believers are *"children of the day: we are not of the night, nor of darkness"* (v. 5).

"God hath not appointed us to wrath"(v. 9). We will not be in this world when God's terrible judgments fall upon this sin cursed earth but will be with Christ in heaven.*"Because thou hast kept the Word of my patience, I also will keep thee from the hour of temptation, which shall come upon all the world, to try them that dwell upon the earth"* (Rev. 3:10).

Verses 12- 13 instruct us as to our responsibilities to our leaders; in verses 14-15 our responsibilities to our brethren and in 16-22 our responsibility to God. I would ask you to notice the order in verse 23 *"spirit and soul and body"*. Man would put body first but the Spirit of God puts the list in order of importance to God. With our spirit we are God conscious, with our souls we are self-conscious and with our bodies we are world conscious. Man is the only living creature that has a spirit.

THE *Second* EPISTLE OF PAUL THE APOSTLE TO THE *Thessalonians*

Introduction

This short epistle is quite in contrast to the first. Paul writes this second epistle to refute a lie that was being circulated among the saints that the *"day of the Lord"* had already come. We have made it quite clear in our exposition of I Thessalonians that the *"day of the Lord"* will not begin until the church is called home. There were those who not only propagated this lie but were so convinced of it themselves that they went about as busy bodies (makebates) and gave up their daily work (ch. 3:7-12). These heretics were troubling the Lord's people by such teaching and Paul desires that *"they were even cut off which trouble you"* (Gal. 5:12; 2 Thess. 1:6).

Chapter 1

Verse 10 *"When He shall come to be glorified in His saints, and to be admired in all them that believe"*. I stand in awe at this declaration. "And is it so we shall be like Thy Son? Is this the grace which He for us has won?" (J. N. Darby, 1800-1882).How these words should humble us, who are such unworthy creatures. *"Sing, O ye heavens; for the Lord hath done it: shout, ye lower parts of the earth: break forth into singing, ye mountains, O forest, and every tree therein: for the Lord hath redeemed Jacob, and glorified Himself in Israel."* (Isa. 44:23)

Chapter 2

This chapter is taken up with the anti-Christ, the man of sin, the beast from [the land] out of the earth. The imitator of Christ who *"had two horns like a lamb, and he spake as a dragon"*

(Rev. 13:11). Many feel this usurper will be a Danite as this tribe is not listed in Revelation chapter 7. In Genesis 49:17 we read, *"Dan shall be a serpent by the way, an adder in the path, that biteth the horses heels, so that his rider shall fall backwards"* Compare this to Genesis 3:15, *"I will put enmity between thee and the woman, and between thy seed and her seed; it shall **bruise thy head**, and thou shalt **bruise his heel**."* How much this beast is like its master Satan, of whom we read in Isaiah 14 and Ezekiel 28. Satan would be as God; he would seek to usurp God from His throne and sit in His place as also will the Antichrist.

Verse 1 refers to the Rapture, *"our gathering together unto Him."* After the Lord comes for His people there will be a great apostasy that Jude warns us of; a great falling away and then the man of sin will be revealed. *"He as God sitteth in the temple of God, showing himself that he is God"* (v. 4).

In verse 7 we have one of the many mysteries that we find in the New Testament which are revealed by the Spirit of God. In the New Testament a mystery is something that was foreknown by God but not foretold in the Old Testament. This mystery is iniquity in its most extreme form. The Holy Spirit will hold this back until He departs this world at the Rapture. It will be after the Rapture that this prince of iniquity will be revealed *"whose coming is after the working of Satan with all power and signs and lying wonders, and with all deceivableness of unrighteousness in them that perish; because they received not the love of the truth, that they might be saved"* (2:9-10).

Chapter 3

Paul concludes his message to the Thessalonians with a reminder of the soon coming of Christ, *"and the Lord direct your hearts into the love of God, and into the patient waiting for Christ"* (v. 5). As much, dear fellow Christian, as we long for the coming of our blessed Lord to take us home, He longs for it even more. Paul's conscience was so pure that he could encourage the saints at Thessalonica to follow him in his pathway. He had kept himself pure before them, working with his own hands as a tent maker to provide for his necessities. He would be an example to those who walked unworthy of the name of Christian and were wasting their time as busybodies stirring up questions as to the day of the Lord and other matters (1:6; 2:2). He would exercise such *"that with quietness they work, and eat their own bread"* (v. 12). If there were those who walked disorderly, they were to take note of such a man and have no fellowship with him, that they might shame him. (v. 14; 1 Cor. 5:11).

The epistle ends as it began, with Paul wishing these beloved saints peace. *"Now the Lord of peace Himself give you peace always by all means. The Lord be with you all"* (v. 16). And on that note I heartily say: Amen.

THE *First* EPISTLE OF PAUL THE APOSTLE TO *Timothy*

In First Timothy we read of some of the characteristics of Timothy. He was Paul's son in the faith. He was tender hearted and moved to tears over matters among God's people. He was of a timid, tender and sickly nature and Paul tells him to *"drink no longer water, but use a little wine for thy stomach's sake and thine often infirmities."* (1 Tim. 5:23). Paul knew his mother and grandmother, who I believe were still alive, which would give us to understand he was a fairly young man. Also in 1 Tim. 4:12 Paul says: *"let no man despise thy youth."* And in 1 Cor. 16:10- 11 in recommending Timothy to the Corinthians, Paul writes *"see that he may be with you without fear: for he worketh the work of the Lord, as I also do. Let no man therefore despise him."*

The proper translation of 2 Timothy 1:2 is *"To Timothy, my dearly beloved child."* Timothy's mother, and I take it, his grand mother were Jewish Christians while his father was a Greek (Acts 16:1). A child was accounted Jewish if his mother was a Jew. From a child he had been taught the Old Testament Scriptures no doubt by his mother (2 Tim. 3:15). Paul had been instrumental in guiding young Timothy in his service for the Lord. Paul had laid his hands upon him (2 Tim. 1:6) imparting, through the Spirit of God, a certain gift to Timothy. We are not told what that gift was but it could have been to overcome this timidity and to serve the Lord without fear (2 Tim. 1:7-8). *"For God hath not given us the spirit of fear; (cowardice)... Be not thou therefore ashamed of the testimony of our Lord, nor of me His prisoner."*

Having given somewhat of Timothy's background and character we now go on to examine briefly the two epistles.

The theme of first Timothy is the house of God in order and the key verse is chapter 3:15, *"But if I tarry long, that thou mayest know how thou oughtest to behave thyself in the house of*

God, which is the church of the living God, the pillar and ground of the truth."

Paul speaks in 1st Timothy of *"the latter times"* (4:1), but in 2 Timothy 3:1 of the *"last days"*. There is a marked difference. The church has passed through the difficulties of *"the latter times"*, which characteristics still continue.

In 1st Timothy chapter 4 in *"the latter times"* the early church was corrupted by false teachers, heretics, schismatics, apostates and legalistic Jews seeking to force the new converts to their legalistics ways. (See Gal.). Note the list of those in the early church and up to the present time who will *"depart from the faith"* (1 Tim. 4:1). In 2 Timothy the evil influences in the *"last days"* are to be moral (2 Tim. 3:2). One has only to read the daily newspaper to see all these things in an ongoing basis. The list concludes with this summary: *"For of this sort* (those found in the list) *are they which creep into houses, and lead captive silly woman laden with sins, led away with diverse lusts, ever learning, and never able to come to the knowledge of the truth"* (2 Tim. 3:6-7). Are these corrupting evils not true of the present day in which we live? Has there ever been a time of such tawdry immorality and the giving up of those things that are pure, honest and true?

So these two things mark the differences between 1st and 2nd Timothy. In 1st Timothy we see the house of God in order but it speaks of the latter times. From the day of Pentecost to now these religious evils manifest themselves. In Revelation chapters 2 and 3, where we have the history of the church given, we read of a departure beginning immediately after Pentecost. *"Nevertheless I have somewhat against thee, because thou hast left thy first love"* (Rev. 2:4). That warmth of love for Christ was waning.

In 2 Timothy we see that the church has become a great house and the *"birds of the air* (have) *come and lodge in the branches thereof "* (Matt. 13:32), evil doctrine. The corruption in the last days will be moral and this character will be manifested just before the rapture of the church.

It is of interest that the salutation, (1:2) introduces for the first time, along with grace and peace, the word *"mercy"*. In the reading of the two epistles one can see why. Note that all the preceding epistles began with *"grace and peace"*. I am continuously astounded at the accuracy of the Scriptures.

How many times is our Lord Jesus Christ referred to as God? In 1st Timothy there are two such cases. *"Paul, an apostle of Jesus Christ by the commandment of God our Saviour"* (1:1) and *"for this is good and acceptable in the sight of God our Saviour"* (2:3).

In 1 Timothy chapter 1:9 we have those for whom the law was made; not for a righteous man. You who would boast in the keeping of the law, would you wish to have your name attached to this list? The law was given to manifest sin, for *"where no law is, there is no transgression"* (Rom. 4:15). *"Sin is not imputed when there is no law"* (Rom. 5:13). *"The law entered, that the offence might abound"* (Rom. 5:20). We Christians are not under the law for *"Christ hath redeemed us from the curse of the law, being made a curse for us"* (Gal. 3:13), but under grace. *"For the law was given by Moses, but grace and truth came by Jesus Christ"* (John 1:17).

In 1 Timothy 3:16 the mystery of godliness is revealed. Again we have Christ's godhead mentioned *"God was manifest in the flesh."* The cross is left out because we are being informed of that godliness which is seen in the man Christ Jesus. The cross was an act of atonement.

Often in the Epistles the doctrine is first laid down and then the practical application of that doctrine is given. This is so in 1st and 2nd Timothy. In 1st Timothy this practical Christianity begins with chapter 5. Fathers, mothers, younger sisters and widows are all listed.

We are enjoined as to how we treat our elder brethren. It has been a very sad experience for me to have seen a number of godly, faithful, elder brothers corrected, silenced and even put out of fellowship. We must remember always that old age brings ways that we might not accept in a younger man. *"Rebuke not an elder"* (1 Tim. 5:1). How important this is in a world that shows little respect for seniors. Further to this we are to *"let the elders that rule well be counted worthy of double honour, especially they who labour in the word and doctrine"* (1 Tim. 5:17). Also, *"against an elder receive not an accusation, but before two or three witnesses"* (v. 19).

In chapter 6 of 1st Timothy we have those things concerning this life and riches. It is not evil to be rich but it is evil to lust after riches. *"The love of money is a root of ... evil"* (NIV). In the closing verses of I Timothy we have some of the most powerful statements as to the Godhead of Christ. *"That thou keep this commandment without spot, unrebukeable until the appearing of our Lord Jesus Christ: which in His times He shall show, who is the blessed and only Potentate, the King of kings and Lord of lords; who only hath immortality, dwelling in the light which no man can approach unto;* (the Shekinah glory of God); *whom no man hath seen, nor can see: to whom be honour and power everlasting. Amen"* (vv. 14-15).

THE *Second* EPISTLE OF PAUL THE APOSTLE TO *Timothy*

Second Timothy opens with Paul's words of encouragement to timid Timothy. Oh! that all our elder brethren would treat the younger so. Paul gives Timothy, his son in the faith, instructions as to his Nazariteship in this world. He is to *"stir up the gift of God, which is in thee"* (1:6); he is to *"hold fast the form of sound words"* (1:13); he is to keep *"that good thing which was committed unto thee"* (1:14); he was to be *"strong in the grace that is in Christ Jesus"* (2:1); he was *"to endure hardness, as a good soldier of Jesus Christ"* (2:3); he was to *"consider what I* (Paul) *say"* (2:7) and he was to *"study to show thyself approved unto God, a workman that needeth not to be ashamed, rightly dividing the word of truth"* (2:15).

One can see from those seven instructions why 1st and 2nd Timothy are called "the young man's (and young woman's) book". Next to John's gospel the young should study and meditate upon the teachings of these two epistles.

In the last chapter Paul also charges Timothy with a very serious charge, for it was *"before God, and the Lord Jesus Christ, who shall judge the quick and the dead"*, to *"preach the word...reprove, rebuke, exhort"* (v. 2). To watch in all things, and endure afflictions, to do the work of an evangelist, even though he might not have the gift of evangelizing. And we Christians, my friends, should take this to heart. To *"be ready always to give an answer to every man that asketh you a reason of the hope that is in you with meekness and fear"* (1 Pet. 3:15).

At the very close of the last chapter of the epistle, Paul gives a list of various brethren. Sad to say *"Demas hath foresaken me"* (v. 10) and gone back into the world. Is it not gracious of God not to leave Mark in the circumstances of Acts 15:37 to 39? For the last time he is mentioned in 2 Timothy chapter 4:11. *"Take Mark, and bring him with thee: for he is profitable to me for the ministry.*" It is remarks such as these that endears Paul to our hearts. What a great and compassionate man of God he was. We see his tenderness and fatherly care throughout the two epistles. Dear older brothers, take heed to this. Your words can make or break a young Christian.

THE EPISTLE OF PAUL THE APOSTLE TO *Titus*

Introduction

I have not much to say about Titus as it is rather simplistic in its theme. It is Paul's pastoral word to Titus concerning various groups of believers: elders, (Paul interchanges this word with bishops, chapter 1:5, 7), aged men, aged women, young women, young men and servants. These instructions from Paul, who had the authority to speak, take up the major part of the epistle.

It would seem that Paul had sent Titus to Crete, an island in the Mediterranean Sea. The Cretians of that day did not have a good name. Indeed this name was synonymous with liar. As the footnote at the end of the epistle says "It was written to Titus, ordained the first bishop of the Church of the Cretians." Paul, who had the power, ordained Titus as he did Timothy to the work of the Lord. I might remark here that we know of no apostolic succession in the Bible. The disciples alone had been commissioned to ordain elders and bishops but when they were gone there were none to ordain. (1 Cor. 7:17; Tit. 1:5). There is a great danger in ordaining men to be elders for it can evolve quite easily into an hierarchy. That is not to say that we do not recognize those godly faithful men among us whom God has raised up and given the gift of eldership and also faithful men who are stewards and look after the business part of the church or assemblies such as the distribution of funds and the preparation and upkeep of the meeting room or church (Acts 6:1-6). Note in this 6th verse *"whom they set before the apostles: and when they had prayed, they laid their hands upon them."* This epistle then concerns itself with practical Christianity and how these various groups are to conduct themselves. *"Works"* is the key word, for it is written that *"ye shall know them by their fruits"*

133

(Matt. 7:16). The word *"works"* is repeated at least 5 times in the epistle: chapters 1:16; 3:1, 5, 8, 14.

We are not saved by works, *"not by works of righteousness which we have done, but according to His mercy He saved us"* (3:5). But then to counter this we have verse 8, *"this is a faithful saying, and these things I will that thou affirm constantly, that they which have believed in God might be careful to maintain good works."* The word *"righteousnesses"* which is found three times in the Old Testament should also be applied to Revelation 19:8 and Psalm 11:7, for in these two cases it is speaking of the fruit of a saved soul.

Chapter 2

Verse 12. Once we are taught from the Word of God then we should live that truth. The Spirit of God does not give us fresh truth if we do not walk in the truth we have been taught. We should be careful *"to maintain good works"* (3:8).

Verse 15. From these words I take it that Titus was a younger man as Timothy was (1 Tim. 4:12; 1 Cor. 16:10). This is a warning to older brothers to treat with fatherly care the younger brothers and nurture them to *"grow in grace, and in the knowledge of our Lord and Saviour Jesus Christ"* (2 Peter 3:18). How much harm has been done by older, legalistic brothers criticizing and discouraging younger men, and nipping in the bud the workings of the Spirit of God in their young hearts.

Chapter 3

"Speak evil of no man... but gentle, showing all meekness unto all men" (v. 2). Oh that we all might pay heed to these words. We may be born meek but we must assume lowliness. Meekness is thinking little of ourselves; lowliness is not thinking of ourselves at all, being selfless.

Verse 8: *"This is a faithful saying, and these things I will that thou affirm constantly."* The literal translation for *"affirm constantly"* is *"insist strenuously"*.

Verse 14. When I was taking my teacher's training in Toronto, another faithful fellow student brought out the literal meaning of this verse for we were all tradesmen in that class: *"and let ours also learn to maintain good works for necessary uses, that they be not unfruitful."* A very practical word. Paul said in 2 Thessalonians 3:10 *"that if any would not work, neither should he eat"*. It would appear that there were those who felt, because of the Lord's promise that He would return quickly, that they would not bother working but were idle, busybodies, walking among the saints in a disorderly fashion. Paul admonishes such that *"with quietness they work, and eat their own bread"* (v. 12).

Paul closes this epistle with *"greet them that love us in the faith"* (v. 15). This and 1 Corinthians 16:22 are the only times that Paul uses the words "Phileos". It is more the word for love in connection with our brethren and family. Agapaos is used in our relationship with God. Eros is never used in the Bible.

THE EPISTLE OF PAUL THE APOSTLE TO *Philemon*

This quaint yet lovely letter was written to an individual, Philemon, in regards to his runaway slave, Onesimus, by imprisoned Paul. He does not speak of his imprisonment but rather twice over that he was a prisoner (bond slave) of Jesus Christ (vv. 1, 9).

His salutation contains the words *"grace and peace"* but the word mercy is dropped for this is a letter filled with grace. This Archippus of verse 2 must be the same as found in Colossians 4:17.

It is not uncommon to find the saints meeting in houses as they did in Philemon's and Aquila and Priscilla's (Rom. 16:5 etc.). Paul's words as to his praying always day and night are not words of social niceties that we sometimes flippantly say to our brethren and then forget about it. We can be sure that Paul meant what he said. He must have been a great man of prayer. (1 Thess. 3:10 etc.).

Onesimus had run away from his master and, in God's divine plan, met in some unexplained way, Paul, who was in prison in Rome. Philemon, according to Paul's words to him and also because the meeting of the saints was in his house, must have been a godly, faithful brother (vv. 2 and 5). It would seem that his home was open to the Lord's people and he was a man given to hospitality. He no doubt was wealthy.

Paul in a most gracious way tells Onesimus' master that he had left him unsaved but now Paul was sending him back not just as a servant but as a brother beloved. We are not told any of the details about Onesimus' conversion but reading between the lines, as it were, it is a great possibility that Paul was used of God to lead him to Christ (v. 10). Onesimus, in some way, had served Paul while in prison in Rome.

Paul felt it was of God to send Onesimus back to his former master and not to punish him for his departure but to receive him as a brother beloved. In time past, before Onesimus escaped, he had been an unprofitable servant. In what way we are not told. But now Paul was sending him back as a follower of Christ and knew he would be profitable.

How gracious Paul is in his words *"I beseech thee for my son Onesimus...but without thy mind would I do nothing...if thou count me therefore a partner, receive him as myself"* (vv. 10, 14, 17). I am sure Philemon's heart melted at Paul's entreaty.

I have always been sorry that Paul felt he had to add these words *"albeit I do not say to thee how thou owest unto me even thine own self besides"* (v. 19). But the Spirit has allowed them to be interjected for some purpose, for every word of God is good and is *"profitable for doctrine, for reproof, for correction, for instruction in righteousness. That the man of God may be perfect,* (full grown) *thoroughly furnished unto all good works"* (2 Tim. 3:16-17).

Paul was assured, as he knew enough about Philemon, that he would do as he asked and even more. The love between these two brothers was great enough that Paul had the liberty to invite himself to Philemon's home knowing that Philemon would be more than willing to prepare him a place.

It would seem from verse 19 that Paul wrote this letter with his own hand, as he did to the Galatians. I believe that Paul had eye trouble and it was difficult for him to write (Gal. 4:15, 6:11). This also would touch Philemon's heart. Paul closes this letter with a salutation from his attending brethren. Luke the beloved and faithful physician, Demas who in time forsook Paul for the world (2 Tim. 4:10) and Mark the writer of the gospel and a few others.

One senses the sweetness of Paul's character in this letter. Also the miracle of a runaway slave traveling all the way from Colosse to Rome and just "bumping into", the natural mind might say, to Paul who was either in prison or in his own hired house in Rome is remarkable and one sees the hand of God in Onesimus' conversion to Christ; but then is not every conversion a miracle? This letter should be an example to all of us to follow the words of Scripture *"finally, be ye all of one mind, having compassion one of another, love as brethren, be pitiful, be courteous: not rendering evil for evil, or railing for railing: but contrariwise blessing; knowing that ye are thereunto called"* (1 Pet. 3:8-9).

THE EPISTLE
TO THE *Hebrews*

Introduction

There has been great controversy over who is the author of this epistle. I do not intend to get into this argument as I am not sure myself. I do recognize that the construction of verses and the manner of expression is somewhat different than what we are accustomed to in Paul's writings. But I am happy to leave this to the experts in such matters. My interest is in the words as this is the Word of God written to the Hebrew saints who were finding it difficult to leave their Judaistic legal laws and ways. The writer seeks to show them that which is *"better"*. I have often felt sympathy for these dear Jewish converts who had been brought up in a very orthodox and strict religion, adhering to the writings of Moses and the prophets. It must have been difficult for them to be brought into the liberty of sons, and to be told that the Old Testament laws were no longer in force but that Christ had redeemed them from the curse of the law (Gal. 3:13). I believe that this is why, in the book of the Acts we see a very slow transition from Judaism to Christianity, from the synagogue to the church and from legality to the freedom we have in Christ as God's sons and daughters.

The writer of Hebrews seeks to show them a better way. This is the theme of Hebrews; bringing these saints out of Judaism into Christianity. The word *"better"* is the key word. It is found thirteen times in the epistle. The other key word is *"covenant"*.

The writer quotes eleven times from the Psalms in the first three chapters: Psalm 2:7; 104:4; 110:1; 145:6,7; 102:25-27; 110:4; 8:45; 144:3; 22:22; 95:7-11 and 97:7. Jews as well as Christians know the Psalms well and so the writer uses them as a link to show these Hebrews *"a better covenant"* than the one made at Sinai (8:6).

Chapter 1

When God sends a prophet to His people it pre-supposes that they are in a bad state of soul and God uses these prophets to speak to His people and warn them of the coming judgment if they do not amend their ways.

But in *"these last days"* God speaks to us by His Son. The Word establishes, in these next few verses, the divine position of His Son. He is the heir of all things. He is the brightness of God's glory and the express image of His person. He upholds all things by the Word of His power and He is much better than the angels. But the most powerful statement from the lips of God is *"but unto the Son He saith, Thy throne, O God, is for ever and ever"* (v. 8, Ps. 45:6). Here we have the Father calling His Son *"O God"* (1:8).

Christ is so much better than the angels (1:4), so much better than Moses (3:3), so much better than Melchizedek (7: 15-16), and so much better than the Levitical high priest (10:11-12).

The word in Hebrew for angel is *elohim*, the same as the word for God only with a lower case *"e"*. It can also mean prince or judge as in Psalm 82. Angels are without number, excel in strength and are God's messengers. There are various classes of angels such as cherubim, seraphim and archangels.

In verse 9 we have a definition of holiness. *"Thou hast loved righteousness, and hated iniquity."*

Christ passed the angels by when He came to earth. *"For unto which of the angels said He at any time, 'Thou art My Son, this day have I begotten thee.'...But to which of the angels said He at any time, 'Sit on my right hand, until I make thine enemies thy footstool?' Are they* (angels) *not all ministering spirits, sent forth to minister for them who shall be heirs of salvation?"* (vv. 5, 13).

It is rather interesting to note the use of the phrase *"Thou art My Son, this day have I begotten thee."* It is used four times in the Bible. In Psalm 2 Christ is called of God to be king; in Acts 13:33 Jesus is called forth to be Israel's Messiah; in Hebrews Christ is begotten or called forth to be God's prophet in these last days; and in Hebrews chapter 5:5 He is called of God to be His High Priest. In Proverbs 8:24-25 there is a similar thought twice enunciated; Christ is *"brought forth"* to speak the Word to bring worlds into existence.

Chapter 2

There are many *"ifs"* in Hebrews. Apostasy was rampant among the Jews in the early church and throughout Hebrews the writer warns them of this: chapter 4:1, 6:4-6, 6:8, 10:26, 12:8. The *"ifs"* of Hebrews are used to test them whether they are real or not. An apostate is one who, though taking his place as a Christian, is never real at all (2 Pet. 2:20-22, Tit. 1:16). A reprobate is one who is disapproved, rejected, castaway (1 Cor. 9:27). The opening verses of chapter 2 refer to this latter condition.

There were many charismatic gifts and acts performed by the apostles at the birth of Christendom. The book of Acts records many of these and Christ told His disciples that they would do many miraculous things (Mark 16:17-18). These were foundation gifts given to the apostles. We see little of them today.

In verses 5 to 8 reference is made to Psalm 8:4-6. There it goes no farther than man put in charge of creation, such as naming all the animals (Gen. 1:26; 2:19). But in Hebrews chapter 2 we are taken on to the second man or to the last Adam. *"But we see Jesus, who was made a little lower than the angels"* (v. 9). I believe it is only here (v. 10) that Jesus is called the *"captain of their salvation"*. This is the place He takes as the leader of His vast army. In Colossians, chapter 3:24 we read *"knowing that of the Lord ye shall receive the reward of the inheritance: for ye serve the Lord Christ."* This militant title is also only found once in the Bible. When we are baptized we, as it were, put on the Lord's uniform. We make an outward show that we have joined the Lord's band.

Verse 12. The Lord speaks of us as His brethren. In John chapter 15:15 Jesus says to His disciples *"Henceforth I call you not servants... but I have called you friends."* What a blessed privilege to be called by Christ His brethren and His friend. James in his epistle, if he is the Lord's brother, never calls him "my brother", nor do we find any of the apostles using this word in connection to Christ. I have always felt that it shows reverence for Jesus' name that there was one Jesus (no doubt his given name) who was called Justus (Act 1:23). *"Wherefore God also hath highly exalted Him, and given Him a name which is above every name"* (Phil. 2:9).

How was it that God could show His heart of love to man? He must Himself take on flesh and blood *"that through death He might destroy* (or annul the power) *of him that had the power of death, that is, the devil; and deliver them who through fear of death were all their lifetime subject to bondage"* (Heb. 2:14-15). *"But thanks be to God, which giveth us the victory* (over death) *through our Lord Jesus Christ"* (1 Cor. 15:57).

Chapter 3

We are four times asked to consider in Hebrews: *"Consider the Apostle and High Priest of our profession, Christ Jesus"* (3:1); *"Consider how great this man was"* (7:4) and *"consider Him that endured such contradiction of sinners against Himself,"* (12:3). A fourth time we are told to *"consider one another to provoke unto love and to good works"* (10:24).

Christ is better than Moses. Moses was a faithful minister of God and like Christ he was a prophet (Deut. 18:15), priest and king (Deut. 33:5). But he was but a servant in God's house. *"Christ as a Son over His own house"* (3:6).

From verse 7 to 11 is a quotation from Psalm 95:7-11. This is in reference to Israel's sojourn in the wilderness when their hearts were hardened against God and provoked Him to judgment. This is another reference to apostasy found in Hebrews. One of many. *"Take heed, brethren, lest there be in any of you an evil heart of unbelief, in departing from the living God"* (v. 12).

Because of Israel's heart of unbelief they were not allowed to enter into the land flowing with milk and honey that God had promised them. From two Scriptures we are given to understand that they never carried out God's instructions. In Stephen's discourse in Acts 7 he says: *"O ye house of Israel, have ye offered to me slain beasts and sacrifices by the space of forty years in the wilderness? Yea, ye took up the tabernacle of Moloch, and the star of your god Remphan, figures which ye made to worship"* (7:42-43). This is a repetition of the same words that the prophet

Amos used against idol worshipping Israel (Amos 5:25-26). It is a warning to those legalistic Jews that mingled themselves among true Jewish believers in the Lord Jesus and sought to bring them back again to be under the law.

Chapter 4

The writer continues the thought of chapter 3. God had a rest then for His people but they were not allowed to enter in because of unbelief. God has a rest for His people today but unbelief can never attain it. There is a better rest for the Christian than Canaan land. *"Come unto me, all ye that labour and are heavy laden, and I will give you rest* (this is for the unbelievers). *Take my yoke upon you, and learn of me; for I am meek and lowly in heart: and ye shall find rest unto your souls"* (this is the rest for believers) (Matt. 11:28-29). There is true rest and peace for the one who is found in Christ. *"There remaineth therefore a rest to the people of God"* (v. 9).

Verse 12. *"For the word of God is quick, and powerful, and sharper than any two edged sword, piercing even to the dividing asunder of soul and spirit."* When one uses God's Word on another it also is used to exercise the one using it; it is two edged.

The subject of soul and spirit is a very interesting one. They are very difficult to differentiate between. Jesus' mother in Luke 1:46-47 prayed *"my soul doth magnify the Lord, and my spirit hath rejoiced in God my Saviour."* Notice the tenses used. The Christian's spirit continuously rejoices in Christ but the soul is changeable. One day it rejoices and the next it is despondent. With the spirit we are God conscious but with the soul we are self-conscious. Man is the only one of God's creatures who has a spirit.

The Word of God is able to differentiate between the soul and the spirit. There are times in the Hebrew in the Old Testament when breath, wind and spirit are inter-changeable. In Ecclesiastes 3:19-21 Solomon, in his sad state, as seeing all things *"as under the sun"* (Eccl. 4:1), sees no difference between the soul and spirit and speaks of man and animals as having one spirit or breath. In verse 21 he goes so far as to claim a spirit for a beast. The beast has no spirit within itself. There is nothing in the whole Bible concerning life after death for animals.

I can understand why there is confusion over spirit and soul. In Hebrew the word for *"breath"* is *"RÛWACH"* and it can mean wind, breath, spirit, etc. (Strong's Concordance #7307). It is found only once in Ecclesiastes (3:19). The word "wind" is the same as that for breath and it is found four times in Ecclesiastes. The word for *"spirit"* is also the same as that for breath and wind and it is found eighteen times in Ecclesiastes. But the word for *"soul"* is different. It is *"NEPAHESH"* (Strong's Concordance #5315). It is found five times in Ecclesiastes and can mean: breath, beast, lust, mind, mortality etc. It has many meanings.

So perhaps we can understand why the words wind and spirit are compared in Ecclesiastes chapter 11:4-5 and John's gospel chapter 3:8. I cannot understand how a Hebrew scholar knows when the same word means breath, spirit or wind. Also I trust that one can perceive why it is difficult to differentiate between soul and spirit.

Verse 14. *"Seeing then that we have a great high priest, that is passed into the heavens, Jesus the Son of God."* Israel had high priests but they never had a great high priest. Christ is better than all the Old Testament high priests. When we come to chapter 9 we shall have more to say about this priesthood.

"For we have not an high priest which cannot be touched with the feeling of our infirmities; but was in all points tempted like as we are yet without sin (sin apart)*"* (v. 15). The blessed Lord knew what it was to be tired, hungry, thirsty in need of sleep etc. Yes beloved there is a true man in the glory, the man Christ Jesus. *"For Christ is not entered into the holy places made with hands, which are the figures of the true; but into heaven itself, now to appear in the presence of God for us"* (9:24).

Chapter 5

The high priest of the Old Testament was taken from among the Levites to offer sacrifices to God not only for the people but for himself. These priests were called of God as also Christ. God called Him forth to be His priest. *"So also Christ glorified not Himself to be made an high priest; but He that said unto Him, Thou art My Son, today have I begotten Thee"* (v. 5).

The Melchizedek priesthood of Christ, which is taken up in more detail in Chapter 7, is introduced. It is said by Bible scholars that this Melchizedek priesthood will not begin until the beginning of the millennium.

Melchizedek is first mentioned in Genesis 14:18. He uses the name *"El Elyon"* or *"Most High God"*. This name for God is most often used in connection with the Gentiles. It seems to be the Gentile's name for God (Num. 24:16; in connection with Balaam). Another example of using *"Most High"* in connection with the Gentiles is *"when the Most High divided to the nations (Gentiles) their inheritance"* (Deut. 32:8). In Daniel 4 it is used five times in connection with the Gentile king Nebuchadnezzar. Remarkably it is not found in Psalm 68 where we have numerous names (8) given for Israel's God. Once again we marvel at the exactitude of the word of God.

The following verses (7-9) give us a very precious insight into the man Christ Jesus. None like them are found anywhere else in the Bible.

No doubt the 7th verse refers to Christ's prayer in Gethsemane (Matt. 26:36) when He sweat, as it were, great drops of blood falling to the ground. I am reminded of Psalm 18, a messianic Psalm. The cross looms large in the opening verses *"the sorrows of death compassed me, and the floods of ungodly men made me afraid"* (v. 4). The Paschal lamb must die but God heard His cry, *"In my distress I called upon the Lord, and cried unto my God: He heard my voice out of His temple, and my cry came before Him"* (v. 6). As soon as Christ had finished the work of redemption then *"He bowed the heavens also, and came down: and darkness was under His feet"* (v. 9). A very beautiful and poetic portion follows describing the Father's haste in gathering His beloved Son to Himself after the work of redemption had been accomplished.

Verse 8. The wording in the King James translation is confusing. The thought, I believe is that at Calvary Jesus perfected obedience. God saved Him because of His piety (v. 7). Jesus was ever and always the perfect and obedient Son. We might say that Abraham fulfilled perfect obedience when he offered his son to God and became the "father of the faithful." The Son of God did not have to learn obedience in the glory with His Father. He had to become a man to do this as John's gospel so wonderfully bears out.

Verse 10. Christ was called an high priest after the order of Melchizedek. Aaron's priesthood was passed on from father to son because of death but Melchizedek's is an unending one.

The writer must sadly remind the Hebrews that they were but babes in their understanding of the things concerning Christ and His eternal or unending priesthood. The Hebrews, having had the Word of God for centuries before the Gentile nations should have been their teachers. But they were but babes when it came to the Word and as babes had need of milk.

The word *"perfect"* has two meanings in the Bible: (1) full grown or mature as here in verse 9 and Philippians chapter 3:15, and (2) having our changed bodies (Phil. 3:12).

Chapter 6

Leaving now these foundational ceremonies and rites, the writer encourages the Hebrew saints to leave this childish state and go on unto perfection or maturity. In Mark 7:3 references are made to the many washings (baptisms) performed by the Jews (I believe there are well over 100 still used by the orthodox Jews).

Verse 4-8. Apostasy is again introduced, *"a falling way"* (2 Peter 2:20-21; Jude 18-19). But the writer is persuaded that these Hebrew saints had not fallen away but rather there was that labour of love which they showed toward His name. We might remark here that it is not clear to whom the writer is writing. Was this a letter to a group of Hebrews dispersed among the nations, to a certain synagogue or assembly of Jewish Christians? We do not know. There is no opening salutation.

Because of Abraham's obedience to the Lord in offering his son, God swore by two immutable things, His oath and Himself that He would bless Abraham and multiply his seed (Gen. 22:15-18).

In the law of God to Israel there were six cities of refuge to which the manslayer could flee (Num. 35:6). Christ is the Christians' city of refuge. "No sanctuary Lord but thee".

When one had offended the king he would flee and lay hold on the horns of the altar seeking safety there (1 Kgs. 1:50). This act was often unsuccessful. But we have a hope that is steadfast and sure and we are encouraged in verse 18 to lay hold upon it. "We have an anchor that keeps the soul, steadfast and sure while the billows roll, fastened to the Rock which cannot move, grounded firm and deep in the Saviour's love." (We Have an Anchor, Priscilla Owens, 1882.)

Chapter 7

And now we come to this enigmatic man, the Gentile high priest of the Most High God (*El Elyon*) who had no father nor mother, without descent or pedigree, having neither beginning of days nor end of life, but made like unto the Son of God. He was not Christ but like unto. The point is that he was not like Aaron whose sons succeeded him in the priesthood, but was a priest forever. Chapter 10 bears this out. Christ's eternal priesthood will be after the order of Melchizedek. It was totally outside the Aaronic priesthood for this King of Salem (peace) is spoken of before there was ever a nation of Israel (Gen. 14:18). God's name in connection to the Gentiles is *"Most High"* or *"El Elyon"*.

"Consider how great this man was" (v. 4). I believe we are free to interpolate these words to Christ. We are told in chapter 3:1 to: *"Consider the Apostle and High Priest of our profession, Christ Jesus"*. And in chapter 12:3 *"For consider Him that endured such contradiction of sinners against Himself."*

Levi while yet in the loins of his father, as it were, paid tithes to Melchizedek who was not of any of the tribes of Israel. We are emphatically told that *"the less is blessed of the better"* (v. 7). And he (Melchizedek) blessed him (Abraham), and said: *"Blessed be Abram of the most High God (El Elyon)"* (Gen. 14:19). *"If therefore perfection were by the Levitical priesthood, (for under it the people received the law,) what further need was there that another* priest should rise after the order of Melchizedek, and not be called after the order of Aaron?" (v. 11).

Therefore we Christians, whether Jew or Gentile, have a better priesthood, a better law (v. 12), a better testament (v. 22), a better covenant (8:6) and a better hope (7:19).

Verse 13. *"For he* (Melchizedek) *of whom these things are spoken pertaineth to another tribe, of which no man gave attendance at the altar."* In other words Melchizedek was not a Levite nor even of Israel.

The point that the writer is seeking to make is that Christ is *"a priest for ever after the order of Melchizedek"* (v. 17). I have been told that this quotation from Psalm 110:4 is the most quoted verse from the Old Testament found in Hebrews (five times).

Verse 19. *"For the law made nothing perfect, but the bringing in of a better hope did."* *"The law is not made for a righteous man, but for the lawless and the disobedient, for the ungodly and for sinners, for unholy and profane, for murderers of fathers and murderers of mothers, for manslayers"* (1 Tim. 1:9). You who put yourself under the law, do you wish to be included in this list.

"Wherefore the law was our schoolmaster to bring us unto (or until) *Christ, that we might be justified by faith. But after that faith is come, we are no longer under a schoolmaster"* (Gal. 3:24). *"And ye shall know the truth, and the truth shall make you free"* (John 8:32). *"If the Son therefore shall make you free, ye shall be free indeed"* (John 8:36).

And so Christ has become our high priest of a new and better covenant, an enduring, everlasting priesthood. Not only that but He is our great high priest (4:14) which was never said of any of the Levitical priests. *"For such an high priest became us"* (v. 26). None other would do for we who have been saved and redeemed by His blood.

Chapter 8

Now the author of Hebrews seeks to tie things together. *"We* (Christians) *have such an high priest, who is set on the right hand* (the hand of power) *of the throne of the Majesty in the heavens"* (v. 1).

The earthly tabernacle was made after the pattern of that which was in heaven. Moses was told in Exodus 39, ten times over that he was to make the tabernacle *"as the Lord commanded Moses."* There was to be nothing added to it nor taken from it. It was a *"shadow of heavenly things"* (v. 5). A better covenant has been brought in *"which was established upon better promises"*(v. 6). The first covenant was not made without fault for it was conditional upon man keeping it and he could not do so.

The covenants that God made with and for Israel do not encompass the church but we come into the good of them. In Jeremiah 31:31-33, we read of the old conditional covenant and the new unconditional one: *"I will put my law in their inward parts, and write it in their hearts"* (31:33). *"In that He saith, a new covenant, He hath made the first old. Now that which decayeth and waxeth old is ready to vanish away"* (v. 13).

Chapter 9

The writer of Hebrews reviews those articles which were found in the tabernacle reared in the wilderness. There was the Holy Place and the Holy of Holies which contained the ark of the covenant wherein was the manna, Aaron's rod that budded and the tables of the law. The last time the contents of the ark are mentioned there was only the law found therein (Deut. 31:26). Christ who is atypical of the ark, could say *"Thy law is within my heart"* (Ps. 40:8).

Once a year, on the day of atonement, the high priest went into the Holy of Holies to sprinkle blood upon the ark for *"almost all thing are by the law purged with blood; and without shedding of blood is no remission"* (v. 22). This was performed once a year for the sins of the people including the high priest. "Once" as compared to "many times" is the basic theme of this chapter comparing the Aaronic priesthood to Christ.

The blood of Christ was shed once for all and all those who are found under the shelter of His blood are eternally cleansed from sin. *"And their sins and iniquities will I remember no more"* (10:17), says our God. The whole Trinity was involved in the blood shedding of our Lord Jesus Christ (v. 14). The apex of

Hebrews is found in this verse *"How much more shall the blood of Christ, who through the eternal Spirit offered Himself without spot to God, purge your conscience from dead works to serve the living God?"*

Now our conscience has rest, our minds have peace and our hearts have joy.

A testament is not in force until the death of the testator. Christ must die in order that this new order might come into effect (vv. 16-17).

We often read of the pattern of things in heaven. This is somewhat of a mystery for it would seem from the Bible that the earthly tabernacle was but a duplicate of the true and original one which is in heaven (v. 23; ch. 8:5). Jesus, the Son of God, has passed into the heavens (ch. 4:14). He need not do this often as the earthly high priest but only once. He is our advocate on high (1 John 2:1). He now appears (v. 24), He hath appeared (v. 26) and He shall appear (v. 28).

Chapter 10

The Old Testament offerings were but a shadow of better things to come. But they were not perfect offerings for they needed to be done often by a high priest who did not continue by reason of death. The sins of an Israelite must be continuously atoned for, by the blood of animals. His conscience never had constant peace. *"For it is not possible that the blood of bulls and of goats should take away sins"* (v. 4). The next three verses are quoted from Psalm 40:6-8. This is a messianic Psalm referring to Christ's coming into the world. Note the repetition of the word *"once"* with *"daily"* and *"often times"*. Christ's offering of Himself and the shedding of His blood need never be repeated (9:28).

Verse 12 has been the subject of some controversy as to where to place the comma, after *"sins"* or, as it is in the King James translation, after *"ever"*. For my part I believe Jesus' sacrifice is once for all, forever. But also when the work of Calvary was finished He sat down at the right hand of His Father in perpetuity. Could we not accept both thoughts? *"Thy commandment is exceeding broad"* (Ps. 119:96).

In verse 15 we have the testimony of the Holy Ghost that the work of Christ has been accomplished. Verse 16 is a quotation from Jeremiah 31:33. This new covenant cannot be broken by man's failure to keep it, as was the old covenant, but God Himself will establish it in their hearts and minds. Note here that heart is put before mind because the subject here is our approach to God, whereas in chapter 8:10 the mind is put before the heart because we must be enlightened before we can love. Always remember that words have their meaning from the context in which they are found.

What wonderful words of rest and peace these are. *"And their sins and iniquities will I remember no more"* (v. 17). Not just buried in the depth of the sea or behind His back but "forgiven, forgotten, forever".

And now with the boldness given to us by Christ we can enter into the holiest. *"The veil of the temple was rent in twain from the top to the bottom"* (Matt. 27:51). Now we can come into the very presence of God and God can come out to us. "The trembling sinner feareth that God cannot forget. But one full payment cleareth the sinner from all debt." (Charles Henry Mackintosh, Christian Truth: Volume 34). Do you know that Christ has made peace for you and me through the blood of His cross. The work is done; nothing needs to be added to it nor taken from it. Christ died for the sins of the whole world (1 John 2:2). *"We trust in the living God, who is the Saviour of all men, specially of those that believe"* (1 Tim. 4:10). If you have not done so, receive Him now into your hearts.

We are encouraged to draw near to God in full assurance of faith and hold fast to our profession of faith without wavering. *"And let us consider one another to provoke unto love and to good works"* (v. 24). Some Christians put the period after "provoke". We need the communion and fellowship of our beloved brethren and as the day of Christ's return for His people draws near we need it that much more. *"Behold, how good and how pleasant it is for brethren to dwell together in unity!"* (Ps. 133:1).

Sadly after such a revelation of what we have been brought into, the writer must again refer to apostasy (vv. 26-31).

We read of very solemn judgments on those who turn from a loving, forgiving God. They have closed their ears to God's gracious invitation to come. I think of the countless children of Christian parents who have known the way of salvation, have bowed their heads with their families and listened to their father reading and explaining the Bible and heard him pray for his children and may have, at one time, made a profession of being a Christian and yet they have given it all up and have lived a selfish, godless life. Peter speaks of it as *"a dog is turned to his own vomit again; and the sow that was washed to her wallowing in the mire"* (2 Pet. 2:22). It would have been better for them if they had never known the way of salvation. In Luke 12:47-48 we read of many and few stripes showing us that there will be degrees of punishment. Oh what will it be for such privileged children who have gained the world but lost the Saviour? God is a God of grace but He also is a God of righteous judgment. *"It is a fearful thing to fall into the hands of the living God"* (v. 31). *"For our God is a consuming fire"* (12:29).

Verse 32-40. The Jews who had embraced Christianity suffered terrible atrocities in the days of Smyrna (Rev. 2:8-10). The Lord took notice of this. They had fought the good fight and there is laid up for them a crown of righteousness (2 Tim. 4:8).

"For ye had compassion of me in my bonds" (v. 34). This is the only personal reference in the whole of Hebrews. Could it be Paul? These Hebrew Christians had willingly given up their titles, their families, their countries to join the brotherhood of Christ for they had the certainty of a much better future in heaven. The writer encourages these down-trodden saints not to give up. *"Cast not away therefore your confidence, which hath great recompense of reward"* (v. 35). They had been taught about the Rapture and were encouraged to hang on for *"He that shall come will come, and will not tarry"* (v. 37).

Verse 37 is very interesting to follow through the Scriptures. It is found originally in Habakkuk 2:3 where there is a slight change in pronoun: *"though it tarry, wait for it; because it will surely come, it will not tarry"*. In Hebrews *"it"* is changed to *"He"*.

The following verse (38) is also interesting in its repetition *"the just shall live by faith"*. In Romans 1:17 *"the just"* is the important word as opposed to all those verses concerning the ungodly surrounding it, such as the barbarians, Greeks, moral Gentiles and legal Jews. In Galatians 3:11 the emphasis is on the word *"faith"*, where law versus faith is the subject. But in our chapter the emphasis is on the word *"live"* as the writer of the Hebrews is encouraging the Hebrews saints not to give up but to be faithful to Christ unto the end.

Chapter 11

God's honour role of the faithful saints of the Old Testament.

What is faith? There are a number of Scriptural verses that seek to explain this word. *"He that hath received His testimony hath set to his seal that God is true"* (John 3:33). *"And being fully persuaded that, what He had promised, He was able also to perform"* (Rom. 4:21). And then we have theses verses in our current chapter. Christians believe the Bible because they believe it is the Word of God. *"For ever, O Lord, Thy Word is settled in heaven"* (Ps. 119: 89).

God is the only one who can create something out of nothing. He spoke and worlds came into being (Prov. 8:22-30). The greatest act of faith in the whole of the Old Testament was Abraham's offering of his son (Gen. 22) and the greatest act in the New Testament is God offering His Son.

A list of these men of faith and their acts is then given. The list begins with Abel, who offered a suitable sacrifice to God, which prefigured the death of Christ. And this report of Abel's sacrifice has been read by countless millions *"he being dead yet speaketh"* (v. 4).

Enoch the seventh man from Adam walked with God, after his son was born, for 300 years. He prophesied of the ungodliness of the last days (Jude 14-15). Because he walked with God, God gave him the foresight to see the Lord's coming at the end of the age. He was one of only two men who did not pass through physical death, for God took him and he was not. (Gen. 5:21-24). He had this wonderful testimony that *"he pleased God"* (v. 5).

"Without faith it is impossible to please Him" (v. 6). There is only one thing that surpasses faith and that is divine love. *"Though I have all faith, so that I could removes mountains, and have not charity* (divine love), *I am nothing"* (1 Cor. 13:2). And so we have this list of men and woman of faith. The verses really need no explanation to clarify the words for they are clear enough. Abraham through his great act of faith is designated *"the father of all them that believe"* (Rom. 4:11). He had such great faith that he believed even if he sacrificed his son that God would give him life once more (v. 19). *"I and the lad will go yonder and worship, and come again to you"* (Gen. 22:5).

We find Jacob at the end of his life leaning on his staff. We know from many illustrations in Scripture that twig, staff, tree often is in reference to the cross of Christ. Jacob, as recorded in Genesis chapter 32, wrestled with an Angel (Hos. 12:4) who undoubtedly was the second person of the Trinity. Jacob had the victory over this Angel who humbled Himself that He might give Jacob a blessing (Phil. 2:8). The blessing was to make him halt all his life and cause him to lean upon his staff. What a beautiful picture. Must the Lord bring a great catastrophe into our lives and take away our strength, our wealth, our children or whatever to force us to lean upon the cross? Yes beloved there are times in many lives when God is forced to do this.

Verses 23-30. Moses is described in the KJV as being a *"proper child"*, in the New Translation as *"the child beautiful"* and in the NIV as *"no ordinary child"*. It has been said of Moses that he spent forty years in the house of Pharaoh learning that he was something; forty years in the backside of the desert learning that he was nothing and forty years in the wilderness learning that God was everything.

Verse 31. I find it rather sad that whenever Rahab is spoken of the adjective is added *"the harlot"*. I heard of a drunkard who was saved who said "I will carry the scars of my life to the grave." But the grace of God is manifested when we read of Rahab in the Lord's lineage for she does not have that degrading designation there.

Gideon, Barak, Samson, Jepthae, David and Samuel were men and woman who had jeopardized their lives for God. And beloved Christians, God is continuously writing up His people (Ps. 87:6). The judgment seat of Christ will bring all that we have done for Christ to light. All our sins may be forgotten but the Lord will never forget even one glass of water given in His name (Mark 9:41). There it is not even cold.

Verse 35. Although there were those who received their dead raised to life again a better resurrection awaits those who died in Christ. And though they received a good report for all their great and good deeds performed through faith God has foreseen a better thing for us.

Chapter 12

This chapter like the 11th stands on its own. It has little about the priesthood nor the tabernacle and the priests of the tabernacle. The first portion has to do with our position as sons and the second section with apostasy once again.

Verse 1. In the KJV the verse reads *"lay aside every weight, and the sin which doth so easily beset us."* It is not speaking about one sin in particular but of sin in general with which we all succumb to from time to time. Sadly there are those who feel that all our troubles, illnesses, etc. come from an angry God who is punishing us for our failures. This is a wrong thought for *"He hath not dealt with us after our sins; nor rewarded us according to our iniquities. For as the heaven is high above the earth, so great is His mercy toward them that fear Him"* (Ps. 103:10-11). There are at least three reasons that God sends or allows these troubles and problems to come into our lives. They are: punitive, child training as in this chapter, pronative, in order to produce more fruit (John 15:2) and preventive to keep us from danger (Acts 9:26-27, 16:7).

Verse 5. *"My son, despise not thou the chastening of the Lord, nor faint when thou art rebuked of Him"*. The Lord loves us too much as His children to allow us to walk in disobedience. *"For whom the Lord loveth He chasteneth"* (v. 6). If He did not correct us it would appear that we did not belong to Him. In one sense we should be very thankful for this child training from the hand of God. It shows His care of, and His relationship to us. Our earthly fathers seek to have us grow into good and honourable men and women. How much more our heavenly Father. One of the blessings in being a father is that in certain ways we can understand God's dealing with us. I recall a beloved friend and teacher speaking on this subject years ago. He said: "When trouble comes don't try to get out from under it but get all the good from it you can." We older ones remember a doctor of the 40's and 50's who told parents to just let their children do what they wished (Dr. Spock), and we know the terrible consequences of this teaching. The Lord is preparing us for heaven. These trials are difficult to take as we pass through them. Some we can scarcely bear but there is always the afterwards time when the result is *"the peaceable fruit of righteousness unto them which are exercised thereby"* (v. 11).

Verse 12-15. We are encouraged to use this chastening as blessing to our souls. To go on in this schoolhouse of God: *"Make straight paths for your feet… follow peace with all men, and holiness."*

Verse 16-17. Once more apostasy is referred to. Esau, Jacob's brother is an example of such conduct. His birthright meant nothing to him and so he sold it for a mess of pottage. He is spoken of as a *"profane person"*.

The following verses compare Mount Sinai to Mount Zion. The former speaks of the law, the latter of grace. *"Sinai, which gendereth to bondage… Jerusalem which is above is free, which is the mother of us all"* (Gal. 4:24, 26).

"For ye are not come unto the mount that might be touched" (v. 18). If they did they would die. *"But ye are come unto Mount Zion"* (v. 22). In verses 22-23 we have the entire company of believers brought before us. An innumerable company of angels (Ps. 68:17), the general assembly and church of the firstborn, that is those who compose the body of Christ and to the spirits of just men made perfect, the Old Testament saints. In Psalm 22:22, Christ says *"I will declare thy name unto my brethren,"* that is the church. In Psalm 22:25 *"my praise shall be of thee in the great congregation,"* the whole house of Israel and finally *"all the ends of the world shall remember and turn unto the Lord"* (Ps. 22:27), all people.

But then we have this beautiful verse (24) *"and to Jesus the mediator of the new covenant, and to the blood of sprinkling, that speaketh better things than that of Abel."* Abel's blood cried out for judgment, Christ's for mercy (Gen. 4:10).

The chapter ends with a warning, in keeping with the character of Hebrews. To refuse to obey the law of Moses was indeed terrible, for which the nation of Israel received double for their sins, but to trample under foot the blood of Christ and count the blood of the covenant... an unholy thing (Heb. 10:26-29) is incomparable and unforgivable. *"For our God is a consuming fire"* (v. 29).

Chapter 13

This awesome epistle ends on an uplifting note. It is a word of cheer and encouragement. Apostasy is not mentioned and there are no *"ifs"* so common to the rest of the book.

There are a number of beautiful verses in this chapter. The book opens with *"Thou art the same"* (1:12) and it ends with *"Jesus Christ the same yesterday, and today, and forever"* (13:8). *"I will never leave thee, nor forsake thee"* (v. 5). What a reassuring word of comfort. *"The God of peace... that great Shepherd of the sheep"* (v. 20). *"What wondrous words are these, their beauty who can tell. Through life and death and endless days, our Jesus hath done all things well."*

A brother much loved, many years ago, gave me this thought: in the 13th chapter and the 13 verse we have 13 words and the word in the very middle is "HIM" *"Let us go therefore unto Him without the camp, bearing His reproach."* Our lives are but a vapour. We do not seek to remain in this world. God has prepared a rest for those who love His Son. But in the little time remaining let us seek to do good and give of what we have and obey our rulers and leaders who have taught us the Word of God (vv. 7, 17) and to persevere in prayer.

"Now the God of peace, that brought again from the dead our Lord Jesus, that great Shepherd of the sheep... make you perfect (or full grown) *in every good work to do His will"* (vv. 20-21). Jesus is the great Shepherd, the good Shepherd (John 10:14) and the chief Shepherd (1 Pet. 5:4)

As we conclude this great and precious epistle may the good, great and chief Shepherd fill your heart in the abounding joy of His eternal love to you.

THE GENERAL EPISTLE
OF *James*

Introduction

It cannot be ascertained for sure if the writer of this epistle is James, the Lord's brother, or not. There are four men so named in the New Testament. In these overviews I have said numerous times that it is not my intention to go into the history or background of these books nor to determine who was the author. I am only interested in what they write. There are many good expositions and Bible translations that delve into these details.

There is a dichotomy of thought in this letter which I will try to explain.

In the first century of the church's history there were literally thousands who identified with this new religion. This world was turned upside down (Acts 17:6). We can see clearly in the Acts of the Apostles the slow transition from the Jewish law being enforced on Christians and the transition from the synagogue to church. If my reader will look at my comments on the book of Acts he will have this explained (Acts 13:14, 15, 42, etc.). There was even a mixture of keeping the Jewish Sabbath and the Lord's Day or first day of the week (Acts 20:7). The letters to the Galatians and Hebrews were written to bring the Jewish believers out of this legalistic system and into the liberty of Christianity.

In Jude we read of many apostates mingling among true believers, and in the First Epistle of John (2:19) we read of these apostates who went out from the early assemblies because they were not real to begin with. They had a head knowledge but when persecution came in they showed that they were not real (2 Peter 2:20-21).

This explanation makes clear that James in many verses is speaking to the apostates in one instance and the next to true believers. It is important for us to see this and to understand the contrast of words written by James. I will illustrate with but one example, but there are others.

The words in chapter 5:1-5 would not be applied to true believers in the Lord Jesus but rather to apostates: *"Ye have condemned and killed the just; and He doth not resist you"* (v. 6). Then immediately following we read, *"Be patient, therefore, brethren, unto the coming of the Lord"* (v. 7 and those following). This dichotomy of language is noticeable throughout the whole epistle.

With this important point entrenched in our minds, that James is speaking to two companies, let us examine this epistle carefully.

James writes, as does Peter, the Apostle to the Jews, to the whole house of Israel; the twelve tribes that are scattered abroad (v. 1).

Chapter 1

This chapter is occupied with *"testing"* and *"tempting."* The way it is put in the King James translation is confusing. Temptation is a ploy of Satan; it comes from within. God does not tempt man. God tests man from without to prove him. Christ was tested but He was never tempted. There was nothing within the Lord to answer to temptation (John 14:30). But He was tested by Satan (Luke 4). The King James version interchanges these two words as it also does with fornication and adultery (Matt. 5:32) which confuses the true meaning of the words.

In all ancient manuscripts James is placed after Acts. It was written before Paul's epistles (45 AD) and is Jewish in character. It differs from Paul's epistles in that there is no salutation. A James is mentioned in Galatians 1:19 and in I Corinthians 15:7, but if it is the same James as the writer of this epistle we cannot be sure. The great theme is works versus faith (2:17). This is no argument against the teaching of Romans (3:27-28; 4:4-5 etc.). In James it is our works as seen by men; in Romans it is our faith as seen by God (Rom. 4:2).

James, although he dwells on our works before men (2:26), stresses in ch. 1:6 that whatever we may ask for we must ask in faith, for *"a double minded man is unstable in all his ways"* (1:8). Verse 12: *"Blessed is the man who perseveres under trial"* (NIV). Hebrews 12:6 says *"For whom the Lord loveth He chasteneth,"* and verse 8: *"But if ye be without chastisement, whereof all are partakers, then are ye bastards, and not sons."* Peter writes, *"Beloved, think it not strange concerning the fiery trial which is to try you"* (1 Pet. 4:12). God often tests us in our daily experiences. I like what a brother once said on this subject: "We are in the school house of God down here. The Lord gives us many lessons, but then comes examination day to see how well we have learned these lessons." Do not grieve, dear brothers and sisters in Christ, when testing comes. It is planned by an all wise and loving God who is "too wise to err and too good to be unkind" (Spurgeon, "Heart's Ease", No. 647).

Verse 13 clarifies somewhat what was written earlier about tempting and testing. *"Let no man say when he is tempted, I am tempted of God: for God cannot be tempted with evil, neither tempteth He any man."* But God may and does test us.

Verse 17: All that we have and are is from The Lord. *"But let him that glorieth glory in this, that he understandeth and knoweth me"* (Jer. 9:24). *"What hast thou that thou didst not receive? Now if thou didst receive it, why dost thou glory, as if thou hadst not received it?"* (1 Cor. 4:7)

Verse 22 *"But be ye doers of the word, and not hearers only."* *"This is a faithful saying, and these things I will that thou affirm constantly, that they which have believed in God might be careful to maintain good works"* (Tit. 3:8).

One of my dear wife's favourite poems is going through my mind.

I'd Rather See A Sermon

I'd rather see a sermon than hear one any day;
I'd rather one should walk with me than merely tell the way.
The eye's a better pupil and more willing than the ear,

Fine counsel is confusing, but example's always clear;
And the best of all preachers are the men who live
   their creeds,
For to see good put in action is what everybody needs.
I soon can learn to do it if you'll let me see it done;
I can watch your hands in action, but your tongue too
   fast may run.
And the lecture you deliver may be very wise and true,
But I'd rather get my lessons by observing what you
   do;
For I might misunderstand you and the high advice
   you give,
But there's no misunderstanding how you act and
   how you live.

—Edgar A. Guest

Verse 27. Many times over when God is speaking to His children in the Old Testament, He tells them not to forget the widow and the orphan for He is in a particular way the God of the widow and the orphan (Ex. 22:22, Deut. 10:18, 14:29, 16:11 etc.). There are many such references in Deuteronomy which bring before us our duty to God and to man. God's moral laws never change from dispensation to dispensation. Man likes to use the word "religion" but the Word of God doesn't. It is found only five times, and three are in connection with the "Jew's religion," Acts 26:5, Galatians 1:13-14.

Chapter 2

Verse one is very difficult to decipher in the KJV. The NIV is much clearer. I believe the thought is that James is speaking in generalities to believers. Christ was able to see men clearly and understand their motives (John 2:25). We do not have that ability. But we look on the outward appearance and show favouritism to those are in high positions or are wealthy. *"Man looketh on the outward appearance, but the Lord looketh on the heart"* (1 Sam. 16:7). Job has very strong words for those who would esteem one over another. *"Let me not, I pray you, accept any man's person, neither let me give flattering titles unto*

164

man. For I know not to give flattering titles; in so doing my maker would soon take me away" (Job 32:21-22).

Please note the use of the word *"brethren"* in this epistle and the occasions when James uses it. The first time is in his opening words to his scattered brethren. The next time is in chapter 1:16 and again in verse 19; fifteen times throughout the entire epistle. It is quite often *"beloved brethren."* Contrast this with his words to those who were apostates amongst them: *"Ye adulterers and adulteresses"* (4:4). Also chapter 5: *"Go to now, ye rich men, weep and howl for your miseries that shall come upon you"* (v. 1). Also in verse 6: *"Ye have condemned and killed the just; and he doth not resist you."* He could not possibly, in these words, be speaking to his beloved *"brethren."*

In chapter 2:5 James is warning those who, because of their own wealth, despised the poor. He brings before them the "royal law," which is to love our neighbour as ourselves. In Matthew 22:39-40 we read *"And the second* (commandment) *is like unto it, thou shalt love thy neighbour as thyself. On these two commandments hang all the law and the prophets."* *"Love one another: for he that loveth another hath fulfilled the law"* (Rom. 13:8). There is a remarkable verse in 1 Corinthians 13:2, *"Though I have all faith, so that I could remove mountains, and have not charity, I am nothing."* Powerful words are these.

It might be remarked that throughout the epistle James refers to the commandments given by God to Moses. The Christian Jews could well relate to these words.

The law is like a chain; it only needs one link to be broken for it to be useless. Galatians makes this very clear. We need offend in only one point to be guilty of sinning in all (v. 10). But, beloved, the Christian has nothing to do with law for we are under grace. Christ took the law and nailed it to His cross (Col. 2:14). We believers walk in the liberty of sons and by that law of liberty we shall be judged.

Verse 13. This is a very solemn verse. Read Matthew 18:23-35. *"O thou wicked servant, I forgave thee all that debt, because thou desiredst me: shouldest not thou also have had compassion on thy fellowservant, even as I had pity on thee?"* (vv. 32-33). God would far rather manifest His mercy toward us than His judgment. *"While we were yet sinners, Christ died for us"* (Rom. 5:8). God's love is ingenious; it goes beyond the letter of the law. *"The letter killeth, but the Spirit giveth life"* (2 Cor. 3:6).

In verses 14 to 26 James seeks to show that our works as believers manifests our faith in God. Fruit for Christ follows salvation, not visa versa: *"This is a faithful saying, and these things I will that thou affirm constantly, that they which have believed in God might be careful to maintain good works"* (Tit. 3:8). God sees our faith; man sees our good works in Christ. *"Let your light so shine before men, that they may see your good works,* (in Christ) *and glorify your Father which is in heaven"* (Matt. 5:16). One of the greatest ruses of Satan is to make us think that we can get into heaven by our own good works when God pronounces His solemn judgment: *"All our righteousnesses are as filthy rags"* (Isa. 64:6).

Chapter 3

"My brethren, be not many masters (teachers)*"* (v. 1). It is a very serious matter and carries great responsibility for a servant of God to teach others. Such a one needs to be much more on his knees than on the platform. First and foremost, this gift is from God (Eph. 4:11). Secondly, one who teaches others must have a spotless life. Thirdly, he must spend much prayerful time in the Word of God and alone in quiet meditation before the Lord. There is only one thing more important than reading the Word and that is meditating upon it. The clean animals referred to in Levities 11:3 were those that were cloven footed and chewed the cud. A divided walk and a heart and life centered on the Word of God are both required.

This chapter is almost totally occupied with the tongue. It is a small member which can spread much good or it can wreak havoc in many lives. We are told to let our yea be yea and our nay be nay, *"for whatsoever is more than these cometh of evil"* (Matt. 5:37). *"And that ye study to be quiet, and to do your own business"* (1 Thess. 4:11). There is much instruction about the tongue in Proverbs. *"The tongue of the wise useth knowledge aright: but the mouth of fools poureth out foolishness"* (Prov. 15:2).

"He that hath a perverse tongue falleth into mischief" (Prov. 17:20). *"Death and life are in the power of the tongue: and they that love it shall eat the fruit thereof"* (Prov. 18:21).

Lives have been ruined, young souls have been warped and the servants of God have been discouraged and turned aside by the cruelty of man's tongue. *"The tongue can no man tame; it is an unruly evil, full of deadly poison."* (v. 8). Oh! Lord use these tongues of ours to spread the good news of the gospel and to comfort and encourage thy people. *"The Lord hath given me the tongue of the learned, that I should know how to speak a word in season to him that is weary"* (Isa. 50:4). *"How beautiful upon the mountains are the feet of him that bringeth good tidings, that publisheth peace"* (Isa. 52:7).

Oh that God's people would write these words on their hearts and engrave them in their minds. *"For where envying and strife is, there is confusion and every evil work"* (3:16). Any believer who has gone through a division among God's people will know what I am speaking of.

Walter Scott wrote the following article:

"Speak not evil one of another, brethren (James 4:11). We have no sympathy whatever with that discouraging character which finds fault. What is needed in these days is to help, cheer, encourage, and strengthen one another's hands. Occupation with evil defiles! There are certain religious periodicals almost wholly devoted to the exposure of error. It may be appropriate occasionally to refer to evil persons and evil things, but an undue occupation with them has a defiling affect. Occupation with good strengthens, purifies and secures the company and fellowship of the God of peace (Phil. 4:8-9). There is an unhappy spirit of fault finding abroad. Controversy and quarreling too are rife. We would most affectionately and earnestly press upon all believers to cultivate a pure and fervent love to all believers.

"People who are doing things for the Lord seem to be a special target for busy tongues. Of course men of grace and gift make mistakes. Who does not! But Oh! in secret wash the servants' feet. Do not make too much of every blunder or mistake you think you see. Do be patient, gracious and kind to an erring servant. The tendency is to find fault and magnify every trivial mistake, and, as a result crush and humble the servant. So, rather cheer him or her on, extend sympathy and love. Pray much for the servant and give now and then an encouraging word and a kind deed."

But let us note the final verses of this chapter. As in so many cases, there are seven in this list. *"The wisdom that is from above is first (1) pure, then (2) peaceable, (3) gentle, and (4) easy to be intreated, (5) full of mercy and good fruits, (6) without partiality, and (7) without hypocrisy." "Wisdom hath builded her house, she hath hewn out her seven pillars"* (Prov. 9:1).

Chapter 4

It is not difficult to detect the different tone in James' language when he addresses the apostates among true believers. We never get the word *"brethren"* in connection to them in this epistle.

James is addressing those who, though mingling among true children of God, had the world in their hearts. This company had the world's good before them and many were rich and sought after wealth. Note the strong words James uses: *"wars, fighting, lusts."* Those who make friendship with this world are at enmity with God: *"Ye adulterers and adulteresses"*. One would have to be blind not to see that James is speaking to a much different company than those he refers to as *"brethren"* and *"beloved brethren"* (1:2, 16; 2:5; 5:7 etc.). We see this division most markedly in chapter 5:6-7.

James pleads with these apostates with a pastor's heart to *"Submit yourselves therefore to God…draw nigh to God…humble yourselves in the sight of the Lord."* (vv. 7-8, 10).

Verses 13-15. When our children were little I bought a trailer. It wasn't very big but the seven of us crammed into it and made many trips to the Maritimes to help in the children's gospel work there. We had pinned on the wall this little verse: "If the Lord will, we shall travel. If the Lord will we shall stay. Learning thus in calm obedience if the Lord will thus to say." I have never forgotten those words though it has been over forty years since we had the trailer.

Verse 14. We oldsters have a motto amongst us that almost all of us repeat. "One day at a time." "*For what is your life? It is even a vapour, that appeareth for a little time, and then vanisheth away.*" Let us then seek to do as much good for Christ as we can while He leaves us here. "*Therefore to him that knoweth to do good, and doeth it not, to him it is sin.*" (v. 17).

Chapter 5

James continues to berate these rich, lustful world lovers in the first six verses of the chapter. See what strong words he uses against them. Perhaps the strongest words are found in verse 6. "*Ye have condemned and killed the just; and he doth not resist you.*" Is it possible "*the just*" is in reference to the Lord Jesus?

Verse 7. Now James turns from the earth dwellers (Rev. 11:10) to his brethren that he speaks of in his opening words (1:2). "*Be patient therefore, brethren, unto the coming of the Lord*" (the Rapture). "*For the coming of the Lord draweth nigh.*" (v. 8). This hope that the believer carries in his heart of the Lord's soon return for His people is the only hope that is spoken of as "*purifying.*" "*And every man that has this hope in him purifieth himself, even as He is pure*" (1 John 3:3).

James puts before the saints their past fathers in the faith. He encourages them to note their suffering, affliction and patience. Job is an example of this and in chapter 42 of Job we see the end result of his patience, how the Lord blessed Job in so many ways. But the greatest blessing of all was that Job was able to better understand God's ways with him and no doubt with all souls. "*But now mine eye seeth Thee.*" (Job 42:5).

From verse 12 of our chapter, James gives his advice as to our pattern of life. Our words should be few and we should avoid the use of oaths in our language. *"Evil communications corrupt good manners"* (1 Cor. 15:33). The Lord Jesus told us not to swear by the earth or the heavens (Matt. 5:34-35), but rebellious man cannot keep even the least of the Lord's commandments. How often have you heard "land's sake" or "for heaven's sake" in direct opposition to the Lord's words? Such is man.

Verse 16. This portion of God's Word has been discussed much and sometimes practiced. I can speak with familiarity on the subject because my own wife was prayed for and anointed with oil by two brothers. She had just returned from the hospital and had terrible pains in her legs that made her cry out on the Friday and Saturday after returning. I sat up with her these two nights because she was in so much pain and agony. On the following Sunday after these two brothers carried out this act upon my dear wife, she was a little uncomfortable that night but following that the pain entirely disappeared.

I know of a number of similar cases. It is not the faith of the ill person that is required but the faith of those doing the anointing. We have a distinct promise here *"the prayer of faith shall save the sick, and the Lord shall raise him up."* (v. 15). I realize this is little practiced among believers as is also the following verse 16: *"Confess your faults one to another, and pray one for another, that ye may be healed."* I believe this act is still in force and is not included in the list of Hebrews 6. These were foundation gifts such as the gift of tongues. *"The effectual fervent prayer of a righteous man availeth much"* (v. 16).

It is very interesting that in verse 17 we are told that *"Elias was a man subject to like passions as we are,"* but he was a servant of God and a righteous man. His prayer was so powerful with God that it was answered in a remarkable way. Is this the reason one sees so few answers to our prayers because we just do not believe? *"And He* (Jesus) *did not many mighty works there because of their unbelief "* (Matt. 13:58).

Conclusion

Our journey through the Epistle of James has presented us with many practical things that we need to lay to our hearts. Let us, each one, be not only hearers of the Word but doers also. May God bless His precious Word to our hearts and minds.

> Oh teach us more of thy blest ways,
> Thou holy Lamb of God
> And fix and root us in Thy grace,
> As those redeemed by blood.
>
> —J. Hutton

THE *First* EPISTLE GENERAL OF *Peter*

Introduction

The theme of 1 Peter is the government of God in the house of God whereas the theme in 2 Peter is the government of God in the world. The key words are *"suffer"* and *"suffering"* which are found 15 times in 1 and 2 Peter. The great difference between the two epistles is that although Christians go through the same trials as the unsaved, they have Christ for them and before them. The unsaved have only the darkness of an eternity where *"their worm dieth not, and the fire is not quenched"* (Mark 9:44). This epistle was written by the Apostle Peter before the destruction of Jerusalem in 70 A. D. by Titus Vespasian and the Roman Legion. In the second verse of chapter 1 we have another example, one of many, where the Trinity is covertly mentioned: *"Elect according to the foreknowledge of **God the Father**, through sanctification of the **Spirit**, unto obedience and sprinkling of the blood of **Jesus Christ**"*

The Rapture is not mentioned by Peter because it is not an act of government but of grace. Faith being tested through our many trials is mentioned 4 times in the first chapter: verse 5, *"who are kept by the power of God through faith"*; verse 7, *"the trial of your faith"*; verse 9, *"the end of your faith"* and verse 21, *"that your faith and hope might be in God."*

The third word that is common in this epistle is *"precious."* Chapter 1:7, *"the trial of your faith being much more precious than gold that perisheth"*; chapter 1:19, *"precious blood"*; chapter 2:4, *"chosen of God, and precious"*; chapter 2:6, *"Behold, I lay in Zion a chief corner stone, elect, precious,"* and chapter 2:7 *"Unto you therefore which believe He is precious"* or *"the preciousness."*

Thus the words linking the two epistles together are *"suffer, faith and precious."* These words give the tone to the epistles.

Chapter 1

The word *"glory"* is found 10 times in I Peter. It is important when reading the Bible that we pay special attention to a word or phrase that is repeated a number of times. The Spirit of God is seeking to impress these words upon us. The first time the word *"suffering"* is mentioned is found in chapter 1:10-11, *"Of which salvation the prophets have inquired and searched diligently... searching what, or what manner of time the Spirit of Christ which was in them did signify, when it testified beforehand the **sufferings of Christ, and the glory that should follow.**"*

I have capitalized these words because they are of extreme importance. The entire Bible is composed of these two great themes beginning with Genesis 3:15, *"And I will put enmity between thee and the woman, and between thy seed and her seed; it shall bruise thy head, and thou shalt bruise his heel."* Undoubtedly this is speaking of Christ and Satan. The Spirit of Christ in one way or another is imprinted on every page of the Bible.

Verse 8: *"Whom having not seen, ye love; in whom, though now ye see Him not, yet believing, ye rejoice with joy unspeakable and full of glory."* What words could be a better definition of faith! We Christians love a Man whom we have never seen because *"hereby we know that He abideth in us, by the SPIRIT which He hath given us"* (1 John 3:24).

Verses 10 to 11: 2 Peter tells us that *"the prophesy came not in old time by the will of man: but holy men of God spake as they were moved by the Holy Ghost"* (1:21). David and all the prophets did not enter into what the Spirit of God told them to write, e.g. *"My God, my God, why hast thou forsaken me?"* (Ps. 22:1). The examples are too numerous to recite.

Verse 21: *"Who by Him (Christ) do believe in God, that raised Him up from the dead."* We believe in God through Christ; Christ has made known to us the love of the Father.

Chapter 2

In verses 5 and 9 we have *"a holy priesthood"* and a *"royal priesthood."* As holy priests we worship, and offer up *"spiritual sacrifices, acceptable to God by Jesus Christ."* As royal priests we are cited for service: *"that ye should shew forth the praises of Him who hath called you out of darkness into His marvellous light."* On Lord's Day morning when we meet together to worship our blessed Lord it is as a *"kingdom and priests"* (Rev. 1:6, NIV) *"and hath made us to be a kingdom and priests to serve His God and Father."* Note this expression, *"unto God and His Father."*

In chapter 2, Peter is writing to the dispersed Jews scattered among the Gentile nations. He is instructing them in this chapter, as to how they should comport themselves as examples of the Christ they proclaim and worship (vv. 11-17).

Verses 19-21: Dear fellow believer, these words are difficult to swallow. But we are told many times in the New Testament that *"in the world ye shall have tribulation"* (John 16:33). Yes, Christians are not exempt from the illnesses and trials of man but as the closing verses of this chapter attest to, we have Christ to comfort and assure us through these trials. *"For even hereunto were ye called: because Christ also suffered for us, leaving us an example, that ye should follow His steps"* (v. 21). Paul desired to enter into this when he proclaimed *"that I may know Him, and the power of His resurrection, and the fellowship of His sufferings, being made conformable unto His death"* (Phil. 3:10).

Chapter 3

Here is a word to the women in Christ. The whole point is that a woman should, as a man should, have Christ as her object. These other things may be necessary but not to be made an object of. Verse 3 has been greatly misapplied. It does not mean a woman should entirely exempt herself from seeking to look lovely, feminine and presentable. For if we applied the verse literally to the 3 things mentioned then it would mean she was not to put on clothing which is ridiculous to the extreme. But rather than be occupied with these things Peter would encourage his fellow sisters in Christ to exhibit a *"meek and quiet spirit, which is in the sight of God of great price"* (v. 4).

I might interject here that the woman's liberation movement has done great harm to these divine principles of a woman's conduct. There is fear among preachers of today to even mention these verses. I knew a woman who took courses in religion at university who said to me one day, "Paul was a woman hater." Nothing could be farther from the truth. See what Paul says about Phebe in Roman 16 and of other beloved sisters in the same chapter . The legalizing pressure by some who would seek to put sisters under law and misuse Scripture has done great harm. The Bible says *"Let your moderation be known unto all men. The Lord is close by"* or *"He is watching"* (Phil. 4:5 NT). This is a great principle to follow.

Verses 8-9: Oh that we would hearken to the guiding words of this Scripture. *"Be ye all of one mind, having compassion one of another, love as brethren,* (literally "be loving as the brethren"), *be pitiful, be courteous: Not rendering evil for evil, or railing for railing: but contrariwise blessing".*

In verses 10, 11 and 12, Peter uses a quotation from Psalm 34:12 but the judgment portion is left out. This is not a day of fellow judgment but of showing grace to all men.

Verse 14: *"But and if ye suffer for rightneousness' sake, happy are ye: and be not afraid of their terror,* (the Gentiles), *neither be troubled."* Indeed if we are faithful we will, in many ways, be ostracized and suffer persecution. The more faithful we are the more we will suffer, of that be assured, but *"if ye be reproached for the name of Christ, happy are ye"* (4:14). The world has no understanding of this.

In verse 18, we again have another instance of the Trinity given covertly. *"For **Christ** also hath once suffered for sins ... that He might bring us to **God**, being put to death in the flesh, but quickened by the **Spirit.**"*

The whole Trinity took part in the resurrection of Christ. Here in this verse, He was raised by the Spirit. In Ephesians 1:20, God *"raised Him from the dead"* and in John 10:18, Jesus said *"No man taketh it from me,* (His life) *but I lay it down of myself. I have power to lay it down, and I have power to take it again."*

We come now in verses 18 to 21, to verses that have been a matter of confusion and bewilderment. With God's help and guidance from godly teachers of the Scriptures, I will try to clarify this. The Spirit of God raised Jesus from the dead. It was by this same Spirit that the Word was preached to them while alive who are now in prison (Hades or Sheol). They were like those of Noah's days when God in longsuffering grace waited for 120 years to draw men to Himself. But unhappily only 8 souls were saved out of the waters of death. This figure of the waters of death into which Christ entered is the baptism which alone is able to save us. Chapter 4:6 helps somewhat to clarify these verses and substantiate what I have just written. *"For this cause was the gospel preached also to them that are dead, (now) that they might be judged according to men in the flesh, but live according to God in the Spirit."* It is ludicrous to believe that the gospel was preached to those who are dead.

Chapter 4

Flesh in these opening verses is seen in 3 ways. *"For asmuch then as Christ hath suffered for us in the flesh* (holy flesh), *arm yourselves likewise with the same mind: for he that hath suffered in the flesh* (sinful flesh) *hath ceased from sin; that he no longer should live the rest of his time in the flesh* (our bodies) *to the lusts of men, but to the will of God."* (vv. 1-2).

Verse 4. *"Wherein they* (the Gentiles) *think it strange that ye run not with them to the same excess of riot, speaking evil of you."* The Jews on the sacking of Jerusalem in 70 A.D. had been dispersed among the Gentile nations. Their ways as Christian Jews were strange to the Gentiles and they suffered persecution and death because of this. It is well to keep this in mind when reading 1 Peter. Peter gives these Jewish Christians guidance in this chapter as to how they should comport themselves. (vv. 8-10). How is it that we can glorify God? Verse 14 gives the answer. Faithfulness will bring reproach but it will also bring joy to our hearts that in some way we can enter into those non-atoning sufferings of Christ.

Verse 18 should read, "and if the righteous with difficulty be saved, where shall the ungodly and sinner appear?"

Chapter 5

This chapter gives a word to the undershepherds, bishops or overseers which are one and the same. It is a great responsibility to be an undershepherd and to care for the flock. Ezekiel 34 is important to read in this connection. An undershepherd is one who has a divine love for God's people. Paul, John and Peter showed this spirit. Peter, in 2 Peter 1:10,11, shows this desire for God's lambs. *"Give diligence to make your calling and election sure."* As another has written, Peter desired that the saints would enter into heaven with all flags flying. John, in I John 2:28, writes *"and now, little children, abide in Him; that, when He shall appear, we may have confidence, and not be ashamed before Him at His coming."* And Paul in 1 Thessalonians 2:19 writes, *"For what is our hope, or joy, or crown of rejoicing? Are not even ye in the presence of our Lord Jesus Christ at His coming?"* Oh to have a heart for God's children as these three beloved apostles had.

In this connection there is an interesting verse in Ecclesiastes chapter 12:11, *"The words of the wise are as goads, and as nails fastened by the masters of assemblies, which are given from one shepherd."* A goad is used to keep the cattle in line and going in the direction that the husbandman wishes them to go. The nails speak of that stability and confidence that a good "master of the assemblies" can impart to the sheep. But it all comes from an ascended Christ; from the *"Good Shepherd."* In Leviticus 25:43, we have a warning to those who would use such a blessed position wilfully, *" thou shalt not rule over him with rigour."*

If as overseers we carry out Peter's instructions as to our conduct and attitude to one another, there will be peace and unity. *"Yea, all of you be subject one to another, and be clothed with humility... Humble yourselves therefore under the mighty hand of God."* (v. 5-6).

Verse 9: *"Whom resist* (the devil) *steadfast in the faith, knowing that the same afflictions are accomplished in the brotherhood* (New Translation)*, that are in the world."* (see chapter 2:17).

Finally, Peter give his benediction to his scattered brethren. Here it is *"the God of all grace"* (v. 10). In Philippians 4:9, it is the

"God of peace" and in 2 Corinthians 13:11, it is the *"God of love."* What a glorious God we have!

Verse 13 has caused some confusion. It should properly read, "She that is elected with you salutes you and so doth Marcus my son." One cannot be dogmatic about it but we know from Matthew 8:14, that Peter was married and these words would suggest that Peter is referring to his wife and son who were with him in Babylon.

I have wondered if Babylon was the correct location given as we never read of any of the disciples travelling so far from their own land as this. Or is Babylon a synonym for another city?

THE *Second* EPISTLE GENERAL OF *Peter*

Introduction

As stated in the opening remarks to 1 Peter, 2 Peter presents to us the government of God in the world. The similarities between this epistle and Jude are so many that it is thought by some that the two epistles were written by the same author. I do not believe this to be so. Many of the verses in Isaiah, Jeremiah and Ezekiel repeat the same sentiments. Also it is important to realize that when God repeats the same matter and words He is seeking to emphasize these thoughts and show that they are of great importance. In Genesis 41, Pharaoh dreamed the same dream twice. He was greatly troubled by these dreams and Joseph was called to interpret them. His remark to Pharaoh verifies this belief, *"And for that the dream was doubled unto Pharaoh twice; it is because the thing is established* (or prepared) *by God, and God will shortly bring it to pass"* (Gen. 41:32).

I always read this epistle with a certain amount of sadness because our fellow men are subject to the same troubles, difficulties and sufferings that everyone is in life but they do not have Christ to turn to for comfort, hope and relief. I will not attempt here to show the many obvious repetitions of the verses found in Jude that we have in 2 Peter. One has only to look in the center margin of any King James translation to see how many times Jude is referred to. Peter is writing once more to the *"strangers scattered throughout Pontus, Galatia, Cappadocia, Asia and Bithynia"* (1 Pet. 1:1). That is to his own national brethren. It is well in the understanding of both epistles to keep this in mind. In chapter 3:1, Peter writes, *"This second epistle, beloved, I now write unto you."*

Chapter 1

The opening words would remind those scattered throughout these numerous countries of the many blessings that God has given to them: *"according as His divine power hath given unto us all things that pertain unto life and godliness"* (v. 3), *"great and precious promises, a divine nature"* (v. 4). Verse 5 should read: "and beside this, give all diligence and have in your faith moral courage." Then we are given a list of seven things we are to add to *"your faith: virtue* (moral courage), *knowledge, temperance* (or self control), *and to temperance patience* (or endurance), *and to patience godliness, and to godliness brotherly kindness, and to brotherly kindness charity* (or divine love)*"* (vv. 5-7). It is remarkable how often when we get a list it is given in sevens. Seven in Scripture is divine fullness or completion.

The Peter of 1 and 2 Peter is not of the same character that we find in the Gospels. I believe his witnessing the crucifixion of Jesus, and his denial of Him and then his personal restoration wrought a great change in his soul. The Lord Jesus in the Gospel of John, chapter 13:36 and 21:18, prophesied of Peter's death and that he too would *"stretch forth thy hands"* as Jesus did on the cross. History tells us that Peter was also crucified, only he asked to be crucified upside down as he felt himself unworthy to die a similar death to Christ. Peter in verse 14 of our chapter willingly accepts Jesus' foretelling of his death and does not argue about it as he did when Christ spoke of His own death (Matthew 16:22-23).

In verse 17 Peter relates the glowing experience that he had on the holy mount when God spoke audibly: *"this is my beloved Son in whom I am well pleased."* (Matt. 17:5). This is another instance of Peter's hasty words and actions when he sought to instruct the Lord to make three tabernacles, putting Jesus on the same plane as Moses and Elijah.

Verse 19: The proper translation of this verse is: *"we have also the prophetic word made sure."*

Verse 20: Men would build a doctrine on one or more isolated verses to the misleading of many. The Word of God is one whole while having the same author even the Spirit of

God through the mouths or pens of various writers. *"No proph-ecy of the Scripture is of any private* (isolated) *interpretation... but holy men of God spake as they were moved by the Holy Ghost"* (v. 20-21) (Job 19:23).

Chapter 2

Apostasy is the basic subject of this chapter as it is of Jude where we have once again seven apostasies. It is well at this point to explain the difference between apostasy and repro-bation. An apostate is one who has a knowledge of the truth but it has not reached his heart. *"For if after they have escaped the pollutions of the world through the* (head) *knowledge of the Lord and Saviour Jesus Christ, they are again entangled therein, and over-come, the latter end is worse with them than the beginning."* (v. 20). An apostate is one who falls away and was never real (Acts 21:21 forsake = *apostasi*), 1 Timothy 4:1, *"...in the latter times some shall depart from the faith."*

A reprobate on the other hand is a castaway, rejected, disap-proved. *"Know ye not your own selves, how that Jesus Christ is in you, except ye be reprobates?"* (2 Cor. 13:5). In 1 Corinthians 9:27 Paul states, *"But I keep under my body, and bring it unto subjection: lest that by any means, when I have preached to others, I myself should be a castaway* (or rejected)*"* (NT). There are so many statements in this chapter about apostasy that are also found in Jude that I shall leave these until our study of that epistle. I count 13 similarities in this one chapter between Peter and Jude.

Verse 7: God knows more about Lot than the Bible tells us when He says *"and delivered just Lot, vexed with the filthy conversa-tion of the wicked: (for that righteous man dwelling among them, in seeing and hearing, vexed his righteous soul from day to day with their unlawful deeds)."* Has the world changed any today?

Verse 20: *"For if after they have escaped the pollutions of the world through the knowledge of the Lord and Saviour Jesus Christ... ."* Pollutions are outward, corruptions are inward (1:4).

Chapter 3

"This second epistle, beloved. I now write unto you" (v. 1) verifies that both the 1st and 2nd epistles are from the pen of the same apostle to the Jews (Gal. 2:7). The last days mentioned in verse 3 speak not of the latter days as 1 Timothy 4:1, but of this time in which we live just before the Lord's coming. In my short life span of over 80 years I have seen that transition from the *"latter days"* where there would be a great departure from the Word of God, a giving up of those moral laws laid down in the Scriptures when every home had a Bible on a shelf, some I fear just gathering dust, but there nonetheless to *"the last days"*. The majority of Canadians were churchgoers and God fearing and the immorality so rampant today was little seen. As most Christians will attest to, we feel that we are definitely in the *"last days."*

Unbelief is rampant among men; the mocking and disparaging of all things Christian is well known. Men walking after their own lusts, uncontrolled lawlessness (this is the definition of sin). They scoff at the Christians' present hope of the Lord's soon return. *"For this they are willingly ignorant"* (v. 5). God's time is not come and the wheels of prophesy grind slowly. In His long suffering mercy God is not willing that any should perish (v. 9). It is remarkable that the man who lived the longest was Methuselah, whose name means "at whose death, judgment." When Methuselah died the floods came. God in grace waited in the days of Noah that souls might be saved but alas Noah's preaching resulted in only 8 souls being saved from the waters of death (ch 2:5; 1 Peter 3:20). Two of the four days explained in our notes on Philippians are referred to in this chapter: *"the day of the Lord"* (v. 10) and *"the day of God"* (v. 12) (the eternal state). There shall be a new heaven and a new earth wherein righteousness will dwell, not reign as in the millennium. (Isa. 32:1).

Verse 15: The Lord is graciously waiting for that last soul to be brought in before His righteous judgment falls with all its ferocity and terror upon this world.

The gracious words concerning Paul show that there was no animosity between these two beloved apostles of the Lord Jesus even though Paul had to admonish Peter sternly and openly for his hypocrisy concerning the Gentiles (Gal. 2:14): Oh that we had the grace to take godly admonition (Ps. 141:5, Rom. 15:14). Peter acknowledges that some of Paul's writings are *"hard to be understood"* (v. 16), but God does not hand us knowledge of His Word on a silver platter as it were. We need to be earnest and diligent workmen *"rightly dividing the word of truth,"* (2 Tim. 2:15). But beloved there are great rewards in the study and meditation of God's holy Word.

Conclusion

There are joys in the path of faith that only the Christian knows. *"Seek ye out of the book of the Lord, and read"* (Isa. 34:16). May the Spirit of God guide my reader to *"search the Scriptures"* (John 5:39). *"But grow in grace, and in the knowledge of our Lord and Saviour Jesus Christ. To Him be glory both now and forever. Amen"* (v. 18).

THE *First* EPISTLE OF *John*

Introduction

The Gospel of John presents to us eternal life as seen in Jesus; 1st John as seen in the believer.

The 1st Epistle of John is the equivalent in the New Testament to the Song of Solomon in the Old Testament. There is the warmth of affection, the relationship of love, the tenderness of expression in both books. The key word which ties the first epistle together is *"children"*.

Let us make a study of this word as it appears in 1 John in the Greek.

TEKNON, TEKNION, PAIDON

Strong's Concordance:

5043 TEKNON — A child, to beget, "my bairnies" (C.W.) It is found in chapter 3:1, 2, 10; 5:2. Four times.

5040 TEKNION — The diminutive of teknon, an infant, darling. It is found in chapter 2:1, 12, 28; 3:7, 18; 4:4; 5:21. Seven times.

5813 PAIDON — A childling, an infant, an immature Christian, to train, instruct. It has reference to growth. Has not the same warmth of affection as teknon. It is found in chapter 2:13, 18. Two times.

The sweetness of the use of the word *"Teknion"* in the Scripture is a subject to warm our hearts.

The first time we are introduced to this word is in John 13:33. For those who use the New Translation as their authoritative source, Mr. Darby uses the word *"children"* but in his footnotes, I quote: "TEKNIA – diminutive; an affectionate term as in 1 John 2:1, 12, 28."

This adjective *"little"* is not to be thought of as condescending. No, not in the least, for then one loses the sweetness of what the Spirit of God is seeking to bring us into in God's thoughts about His people."

In 1 John chapter 2, we have the three stages of man: little children, young men and fathers. In verse 12 the word used is *"Teknion"* because it is including all God's children. But in the second instance (v. 13) there is the thought of growth and a different word is used which is also the diminutive, *"Paidon"*. In 1 John 3:1-2 where we have *"sons of God"* in the King James version the New Translation rightly has *"children of God"*. The word *"Teknion"* is used in this case as it also is in the 10th verse.

The perfection of the Word of God is shown out when we see the seven places where the Spirit of God uses the diminutive *"Teknion"* and the other places where He uses the word *"Teknion"*. When the word *"Teknon"* is used it is more in the abstract, that is, it is the pronouncement that there is relationship but not the same intensity of affection and dependence as when *"Teknion"* is used.

For example, someone might ask me "whose daughter is that girl" and I would answer "she is my child" (*Teknon*). But if that same daughter is passing through trials or in some situation where she needs the assurance of my affection and care for her, I might say "my little child" (*Teknion*) I want you to know I am always near to help when you need me." Perhaps again someone may speak of my daughter affectionately, as to some kindness she has shown, and I might say "Yes that is my little child" (*Teknion*) even though she may be fully grown. One can perceive in these feeble examples that the use of the word "little" is in no way condescending nor suggests inferiority as one might use the word "little" when describing some object, e.g. "that farmer's apples are so little" or seeking to disparage another person, e.g. "he is such a little person, really".

The King James Version and New Translation have been used in meditating upon this heart-warming subject. The footnote to John 13:33 has already been quoted above but the footnote to 1 John 2:1, in the NT of the exact same word is *"Teknion"* (a diminutive). It is a term of parental affection. It applies to Christians irrespective of growth (contrasted with *Paidon*). Used in verses 2:1, 12, 28; 3: 7, 18; 4:4; 5:21; John 13:33; Galatians 4:19.

To help those who would enter into the enjoyment of the word *"Teknion"* following are all of the cases (9) where this word is found as well as the few where the words *"Teknon"* and *"Paidon"* are found. The generally used King James version is quoted.

Teknion (Diminutive)

John 13:33 *"Little children, yet a little while I am with you."* He was going away and they were sad.

Galatians 4:19 *"My little children, of whom I travail in birth."* Paul had spoken strongly to the Galatian saints who needed to be corrected but now his affection for them shines out.

1 John 2:1 *"My little children, these things I write unto you, that ye sin not."*

1 John 2:12 *"I write unto you, little children, because your sins are forgiven you for His name's sake."*

1 John 2:28 *"And now, little children, abide in Him."*

1 John 3:7 *"Little children, let no man deceive you."*

1 John 3:18 *"My little children, let us not love in word, neither in tongue; but in deed and in truth."*

1 John 4:4 *"Ye are of God, little children."*

1 John 5:21 *"Little children, keep yourselves form idols."*

Please note in what connection the Spirit uses this word *Teknion* and why *Teknon* is not used.

Teknon (not diminutive)

1 John 3:1 *"Behold, what manner of love the Father hath bestowed*

upon us, that we should be called the sons (New Translation, children) *of God."*

1 John 3:2 *"Beloved, now are we the sons* (New Translation, children) *of God. "*

1 John 3:10 *"In this the children of God are manifest, and the children of the devil."*

1 John 5:2 *"By this we know that we love the children of God, when we love God, and keep His commandments."*

2 John 1 *"The elder unto the elect lady and her children."*

2 John 4 *"I rejoiced greatly that I found of thy children walking in truth."*

2 John 13 *"The children of thy elect sister greet thee."*

One can see from the above list that *"Teknon"* does not transmit the same warmth of affection in the relationship that the examples for *"Teknion"* do.

Paidon

There are only 2 examples.

1 John 2:13 *"I write unto you, little children, because ye have known the Father."*

1 John 2:18 *"Little children, it is the last time: and as ye have heard that antichrist shall come."*

The word *"Paidon"* has reference to growth. I trust that this will be of help to all who read this to a fuller enjoyment of the lovely word *"Teknion"*. I continue to be astounded at the absolute perfection of the Word of God.

I would only add this that I believe the word *"Abba"* relates in a paternal way to the word *"Teknion"*. The first time *"Abba"* is used is in Mark 14:36 when the Lord Jesus was passing through His night of passion in the garden and as the *"terrors of death"* compassed Him about, He cried out *"Abba, Father"*. We find it used appropriately, the next time, in Romans 8:15 in connection with our relationship as sons to the Father and lastly in Galatians 4:6 where the whole Trinity is used in connection with our sonship. Paul only used the word *"Teknion"* once and *"Abba"* twice in all his writings and both words are found in the Epistle to the Galatians. One can understand why he used them there for he is speaking to them as a father.

In John's gospel we see eternal life as seen in Christ but in John's 1st epistle we see eternal life as seen in the believer. Jesus not only imparts unto us eternal life but He is this in Himself. The epistle begins and ends with this truth: chapter 1:2 *"For the life was manifested, and we have seen it, and bear witness, and show unto you that eternal life, which was with the Father, and was manifested unto us."* And chapter 5:20 *"...His Son Jesus Christ. This is the true God, and eternal life."*

The sun in the heavens is a beautiful picture of the Son of God. It sends forth life, light, warmth, power and yet it is never diminished in any respect. So also is the Son of God.

As we are told twice over that Jesus is *"eternal life"*, we are also told twice just who God is. *"God is love"* (ch. 4:8, 16). I believe it is of note that this description of who God is, is given twice whereas we are only told once that *"God is light"*. His love and mercy supersede His judgments, (Jas. 2:13). God's love is ingenious, it goes beyond the letter of the Law.

The 1st Epistle of John is distinctive in one very prominent and obvious sense. It is filled with imperatives or absolutes. Just notice the emphatic statements and contrasts throughout the whole epistle.

The following is not a complete list:

- One is either a child of God or a child of the devil (3:8, 9, 10).
- *"Whosoever denieth the Son, the same hath not the Father: (but) he that acknowledgeth the Son hath the Father also"* (2:23).
- *"Now are we the sons* (children) *of God..."* (3:2).
- *"They are of the world...Ye"* (4:5-6).
- *"Every one that loveth is born of God... he that loveth not knoweth not God"* (4:7-8).

- *"He that hath the Son hath life; and he that hath not the Son of God hath not life"* (5:12).

Here are some of the examples where *"we know"* is found numerous times in the epistle.

- *"And hereby we do know that we know Him, if we keep His commandments"* (2:3).
- *"Hereby know we that we are in Him"* (2:5).
- *"We know that it is the last time"* (2:18).
- *"Ye know all things"* (2:20).
- *"I have not written unto you because ye know not the truth, but because ye know it"* (2:21).
- *"Ye know that everyone that doeth righteousness is born of Him"* (2:29).
- *"We know that, when He shall appear, we shall be like Him"* (3:2).
- *"Ye know that He was manifested to take away our sins"* (3:5).
- *"We know that we have passed from death unto life, because we love the brethren"* (3:14)
- *"Ye know that no murderer hath eternal life"* (3:15).
- *"Hereby we know that we are of the truth"* (3:19).
- *"Hereby we know that He abideth in us"* (3:24).
- *"Hereby know ye the Spirit of God"* (4:2).
- *"Hereby know we the Spirit of truth, and the spirit of error"* (4:6).
- *"Hereby know we that we dwell in Him, and He in us"* (4:13).
- *"By this we know that we love the children of God, when we love God"* (5:2).
- *"These things have I written unto you that believe on the name of the Son of God; that ye may know that ye have eternal life"* (5:13).
- *"We know that we have the petitions that we desired of Him"* (5:15).
- *"We know that whosoever is born of God sinneth not"* (5:18).

- *"We know that we are of God"* (5:19).
- *"And we know that the Son of God is come...that we may know Him that is true, and we are in Him that is true"* (5:20).

I will not attempt to count the numerous times we find the word *"know"* for there are others. But I trust after reading the above lengthy list you will see why I call the 1st Epistle of John "empirical".

Other common words that are found in 1ˢᵗ John:

1. *Commandments,* 7 times. The word has a different meaning from the Hebrew word "Commandment" that we find in the Old Testament.

2. *Love,* 34 times. It is either *"agape"* or *"phileos"* but never *"eros"*. Eros is never found in the original Greek. It is a fleshy physical love. Eros I believe was the mythical son of the goddess Diana, the goddess of love. Occasionally God uses the word *"phileos"* but most often *"agape"*. It is interesting and instructive to note the Bible's use of the two words. Note its use in John 3:35. *"The Father loveth (agapos) the Son."* But in John 5:20 when the Jews sought to kill Jesus, the word *"phileos"* is used. My notes on *"Teknion"* and *"Teknon"* give an illustration of perhaps why God the Father uses two different words in these two Scriptures. A very sweet difference.

   Then again in John 21:14-17 in the Lord's conversation with Peter, Jesus the first two times that He seeks the assurance of Peter's love uses the higher form of the word. Peter always answers with *"Lord thou knowest that I love (phileos: attached) Thee."* The third time Jesus asks Peter He adopts Peter's word. Peter had denied Jesus three times. *"Agapaos"* is the word that God generally uses. It has a higher, more spiritual meaning, whereas *"phileos"* is a more natural love, yet pure and not as *"eros"*. In English we use the root word as *filial, philadelphia,* brotherly love.

3. *Eternal life,* 6 times.

4. *Father,* 15 times.

5. *Spirit,* 12 times.

6. *Abide,* 3 times

Conclusion

The key words in 1st John are: *hath, know, children, Father, Spirit, love, abide* and *eternal life.*

There is also one other important fact we must keep in mind when studying John's 1st epistle. That is that John speaks of the two natures, the old, which we are born with and the new, which we receive when we accept Christ as our Redeemer and Lord. The old nature is Adamic and has no good in it at all (Rom. 7:18). This is why we need an advocate (2:1). Also *"if we say that we have no sin, we deceive ourselves, and the truth is not in us"* (1:8). On the other hand the new nature is born of God and cannot sin (3:6-10). Understanding these two natures make the above comments clear.

Another wondrous point that John emphasizes is that the Spirit of God which abides in every believer gives us the knowledge:

1. that He abides in us (3:24),

2. that we dwell in Him (4:13), and

3. that we have the witness in ourselves that Jesus is the Son of God (5:10).

Three blessed and extremely important truths.

It was not my intention in this study to go through this epistle verse by verse but rather bring to the readers' attention the heart of what John was seeking to bring before us in this lovely family epistle. Like Hebrews, but unlike the epistles of Paul, there is no salutation. It is to the whole family of God to give to us the certain knowledge of what we have in Christ and our connection to Him and to one another.

He lives in us; we live in Him.
We are from God.
We are born of God.
We have eternal life now as a present possession.
We have overcome the world.
We live in the light and shall live forever.
We have the Father.
We are, right now, God's children.
We are going to be like Him when we see Him.
We have passed from death unto life.
We know that He hears us… whatever we ask.
We know that we are His children.
ALLELUJAH !

THE *Second* EPISTLE OF *John*

The 1st epistle is written to the children, the 2nd is written to "*the elect lady*" and the 3rd, to the elder Gaius. In the second epistle, Christians are enjoined not to company nor have anything to do with those who would seek to corrupt the truth by bringing in false doctrine among God's children. They are called "*deceivers*" (v. 7). We are not to receive such into our houses nor even wish them good-bye (god-speed) (v. 10). For if we do we become corrupted also and become "*partakers of his evils deeds*"(v. 11).

THE *Third* EPISTLE
OF *John*

In the 3rd epistle, on the other hand, John encourages us to open our doors and hearts to those who are Christ's servants. *"We therefore ought to receive such"* (v. 8). Two men are brought before us besides Gaius whose names begin with "D". One is *"Diotrephes"* (v. 9) who loved to have the chief place and lord it over God's people as the pharisees did and rule unjustly. But then we have *"Demetrius"* who had a *"good report of all men, and of the truth itself "* (v. 12). We thank God for these men amongst us, fatherly, kindly, wise in the faith. But sadly, and too often, there are those who take control and overrule, not only the assembly but those who are of a softer, gentler nature. 1 Peter 5:1-5 and Proverbs 27:23-27 gives us the lovely character of these "undersheperds" and Hebrews 13 guides us to *"remember them which have the rule over you, who have spoken unto you the Word of God"* (v. 7). And again in verse 17 *"obey them that have the rule over you, and submit yourselves"*.

Well dear reader I trust this is enough to wet your spiritual appetite to dig deep into these blessed portions of God's Word. Truly, J. N. Darby said "the cream is on the surface, but you have to dig for the nuggets."

THE GENERAL EPISTLE
OF *Jude*

The epistle of Jude in the New Testament is the Malachi of the Old. There are seven fallings away or apostacies in each. Its theme is apostasy or the falling away from the path of truth as found in the Bible. If you will read the comment on 2 Peter, the difference between an apostate and a reprobate is explained. 2 Peter and Jude are much alike in content. When we turn the grace of God into lasciviousness it results in apostasy.

In the early church, after the ascension of Christ, and even though there was a great persecution of the Christians, there were thousands aligning themselves with this new religion. Many of them slipped in unawares and were not true at all. They had *"a form of godliness, but denying the power thereof"* (2 Tim. 3:5). In Jude these false disciples come in, in great numbers seeking to corrupt the truths of Scripture (v. 4), but in the 1st Epistle of John, they go out (1 John 2:19). In John's gospel, chapter 6, many were offended by Jesus' words in regard to eating His flesh and drinking His blood (John 6:54). They said, *"this is a hard saying; who can hear it"* (John 6:60). In verse 66 of this same chapter it says *"from that time many of His disciples went back, and walked no more with Him"*. They were not real to begin with.

It is of great interest to notice the salutations in all the epistles. The words *"grace and peace"* are used in the opening salutations of all the epistles until 1st Timothy where the word *"mercy"* is introduced. In Jude the salutation drops the word *"grace"* and the words *"mercy and love"* are added. This is the only salutation where the word *"love"* is used and it was certainly needed considering the subject of this epistle. There is but one chapter in Jude but how extremely important this subject is in these last days of the church's history where on every hand there is a giving up of the *"old paths"* (Jer. 6:16) and a falling away from the teachings of the Bible.

201

In the opening we are urged to *"earnestly contend for the faith which was once delivered unto the saints"* (v. 3). Jude, as Peter (2 Peter 1:12-13), would bring before the saints those things they had been taught by faithful men and bring to their remembrance their words to them (v. 5).

I will list the seven apostasies that are enumerated in this epistle:

1. verse 5, the children of Israel.
2. verse 6, the angels that fell.
3. verse 7, Sodom and Gomorrah.
4. verse 8, filthy dreamers.
5. verse 9, Satan.
6. verse 15, the ungodly.
7. verse 18, mockers.

Here are just a few brief remarks about these apostasies:

1. verse 5: There were many unbelievers among the Israelites after they left Egypt. They rebelled against Moses, the servant of God, and were destroyed (Num. 16:32-35).

2. verse 6: It is thought that the *"angels that left their habitation and kept not their first estate or principality"* is referring to those heavenly beings in Genesis 6:2 who *"saw the daughters of men that they were fair; and they took them wives of all which they chose"*.

3. and 4. verses 7-8: So*dom and Gomorrha* is synonymous with that which is rampant today, homosexuality. When I was a boy, homosexuality, though it was undoubtedly practiced, was rarely heard of. In this day it is flaunted even to the parading of half naked men down the streets of our cities. This is what *"strange flesh"* means. *"Filthy dreamers defile the flesh, despise dominion, and speak evil of dignities."*

In the 19th century schools of religious thought emerged which are known as the higher critics. These men supposed themselves to have more knowledge than God and twisted the Scripture to their own destruction. This character also is highly prevalent today and all about us are those who seek to *"wrest, as they do also the other Scriptures, unto their own destruction"* (2 Peter 3:16).

5. verse 9: *"Satan"* (v. 9): Michael used much discretion in not getting into a disputation with Satan over the body of Moses but left that to God. And we should do the same with all the evil that is about us today. *"Let the potsherd strive with the potsherds of the earth"* (Isa. 45:9). Fellow Christians do not embroil yourselves in the religious questions of this world but leave it all to God. *"Vengeance is mine; I will repay, saith the Lord"* (Rom. 12:19) .

6. verse 15: *"The ungodly"*. It is remarkable that the 7th man from Adam prophetically foresaw the day in which we live. The word *"ungodly"* is emphasized by being repeated 4 times in verse 15. Was there ever a day in man's history when there was more ungodliness in the world than today? Everyone doing that which is right in their own eyes (Judg. 17:6; Prov. 12:15, 21:2). Enoch is typical of the Rapture for God took him to heaven or raptured him, *"and Enoch walked with God: and he was not; for God took him"* (Gen. 5:24). He was the father of Methuselah whose name means "at whose death — judgment." The year Methuselah died the floods came. The church will very soon be raptured and then God's terrible judgment will fall upon this world.

7. verse 18: *"Mockers"*. Have we seen more ridiculing of the Bible and of our Lord Jesus Christ than today? The things that are said about our Saviour in the daily newspapers would never be said about Mohammed or Confucius or any of the world's idols for fear of retribution. But the most abominable things are published in all the periodicals of today demeaning Christ and seeking to make Him to be as every other man. "The Da Vinci Files" is a case in point. We Christians are to have nothing to do with these works of darkness and not even discuss them. (Eph. 5:11-12) *"And have no fellowship with the unfruitful works of darkness, but rather reprove (expose) them. For it is a shame even to speak of those thing which are done of them in secret."*

Verse 11: *"Woe unto them! for they have gone in the way of Cain,* (natural religion) *and ran greedily after the error of Balaam for reward, and perished in the gainsaying of Core* (Korah, rebellion)." Again how much are these things characteristic in this our day and sad to say even found among those who call themselves ministers of the gospel.

My dear Christian brothers and sisters, how sad it is to write and read about such an ungodly condition of things in relationship to our day. But, *"Be not deceived; God is not mocked: for whatsoever a man soweth, that shall he also reap. For he that soweth to his flesh shall of the flesh reap corruption; but he that soweth to the Spirit shall of the Spirit reap life everlasting"* (Gal. 6:7-8). But our business is to *"turn to God from idols to serve the living and true God; and to wait for His Son from heaven, whom He raised from the dead, even Jesus, which delivered us from the wrath to come"* (1 Thess. 1:9-10).

From verses 20 to 25, we have Jude's closing instruction. *"But ye, beloved, building up yourselves on your most holy faith,* (edification), *praying in the Holy Ghost* (supplication), *keep yourselves in the love of God* (preservation), *looking for the mercy of our Lord Jesus Christ unto eternal life* (anticipation)." These are four things, among others, that will preserve us in this evil day: edification, supplication, preservation and anticipation. In Romans 8:30, we find the culmination of all these; our coronation, *"Moreover whom He did predestinate, them He also called: and whom He called, them He also justified: and whom He justified, them He also glorified."* May we labour on, beloved, keeping the end of our faith in sight.

"Now unto Him that is able to keep you from falling, and to present you faultless before the presence of His glory with exceeding joy, to the only wise God our Saviour, be glory and majesty, dominion and power, both now and ever. Amen" (vv. 24-25).

THE *Revelation* OF JESUS CHRIST

Note: In many Bibles the title is "The Revelation of St. John the Divine". But it should read: "The Revelation of Jesus Christ."

Chapter 1

There is a special blessing for all who read this book (v. 3). We read of the One who was from eternity, the Eternal One (vv. 4, 8, 11, 17, 18). In this chapter the Ancient of days is Christ. But in Daniel 7:13 it is God Revelation is divided into 3 parts:

"The things which Thou has seen" (ch. 1).

"The things which are" (ch. 2 and 3).

"The things which will be hereafter" (ch. 4 to the end).

Chapter 2 *&* 3

The seven churches in Asia:

1. EPHESUS: Desirable. The beginning of the church after Pentecost until the 2nd century.

2. SMYRNA: Myrrh. This was the church which passed through the Roman persecutions, in the 2nd and 3rd centuries. Myrrh must be crushed to get the sweet odour.

3. PERGAMOS: Married and elevated. The church made a world institution by Constantine: 4th Century.

4. THYATIRA: Continual offering. The political church formed by bishops and popes. Note verse 19.

5. SARDIS: Remnant. Came out of Thyatira. Protestantism (v. 2:24). "The rest" .

6. PHILALEPHIA: Brotherly love. Those who are real. Who have "kept My Word, and hast not denied My name" (3:8). They will be raptured before the 7 years of tribulation begins (v. 10).

7. LAODICEA: The rights of the People. The final form the universal church will take before the Rapture (3:14). The last four churches will go on until the Rapture. Revelation is only about the last 3½ years. The Rapture is not mentioned, but implied in chapters 4 and 5, as we see the saints in heaven concerned about the earthly saints.

Chapter 4

The subject is *"The throne"*. See how many times the throne is mentioned (v. 6). *"Sea of glass"*, fixed purity. See also chapter 15:2. *"Holy, holy, holy"*, verse 8 is called the "Trisagion". Also Isaiah 6:3. Thrice Holy God. *"Beasts"* verse 6 should be *"living creatures"* (Ezek. 1:5).

Chapter 5

The subject is *"The book"*. See how many times the book is mentioned? The Lamb is named 4 times. Please note the wrong pronouns used in verses 9-10. It should be "them" "they" instead of "us" and "we". It is the heavenly, redeemed company singing about the earthly saints. (See the New Translation and NIV). Chapter 4 and 5 are primarily a heavenly scene and sit between the history of the 7 churches and the things which shall be hereafter (1:19).

Chapter 6

The beginning of the chapters on the judgments of God on this world in the last half of the 7 years of tribulation; the time of Jacob's trouble (Jer. 30:7; Matt. 24:21). There are 4 horsemen. We should not try to define who the riders are but rather what they characterize. The opening of the 7 seals co-join with the 4 horsemen.

1. The white horse. White speaks of peace but it is a false peace and false contracts between nations which will be broken in the middle of the tribulation period (Isa. 28:15,18). *"He that sat on him had a bow"* (v. 2). This is war at a distance. The first 3½ years of the tribulation will be marked by false prosperity and peace. The confederation and pacts

between nations will be broken in the middle of Daniel's seven heptas of weeks, (Dan. 9:25-27).

2. The second seal and the red horse (vv. 3-4) marks the beginning of Jacob's trouble. Peace will be taken from the earth and there will be much blood shed – red. Now there is a sword not a bow, this speaks of warfare close at hand.

3. The third seal and the black horse (vv. 5-6). Black designates famine and pestilence. When artists depict such, with death riding on it, the horse is always black. The rider has a pair of balances in his hand. The poor will suffer the most, wheat and barley, but the rich at this time have little oil and wine. (See Lam. 5:10; Ezek. 14:21).

4. The fourth seal and the fourth horse, a pale one – death. The one who sat on the pale horse is death and hell; death or the grave, where the body goes; hell or more precisely, *Hades* (Greek) or *Sheol* (Hebrew), the place of departed spirits or the unseen world. See Rev. 20:14. Both will finally be cast into the lake of fire. Unfortunately the King James version uses the word hell for hades and *sheol*. The word hell as we use it today does not mean the above but the lake of fire. Gahenna is the final place of the damned (Isa. 30:33). Gahenna is called Tophet here (2 Kgs. 23:10). Tophet is found in the valley of Hinnom from which the word Gahenna is derived. The valley of Hinnom is to the very south of Jerusalem and it was where the residents of Jerusalem threw their garbage and the bodies of dead criminals. Judas hung himself on the hill of Hinnom. But the rope broke and his body plummeted into the valley (Acts 1:18). Mark 9:43, 46, 48 refers to this place. There is no one in Gahenna as yet, but many in Hades (Hell in the King James version). The beast and false prophet of Rev. 13 will be the first to be cast alive into this lake of fire (Rev. 19:20-21).

5. Now we go on to the 5th and 6th seals. Under the 5th seal we see those of the godly remnant who will be martyred for Christ. They must wait for their brethren who also will be martyred. They will be part of the first resurrection.

6. Under the 6th seal there will be cataclysmic happenings that will shake the entire world. Sun is a major power, moon is a power that receives its authority from the supreme power, stars are lesser powers. The western hemisphere is where Christianity has prevailed but has apostatized (2 Tim. 3:1-7; Jeremiah 25:29-33). Before the 7th seal is introduced in ch. 8:1, a parenthetical chapter comes in.

Chapter 7

Note the use of number four in v 1. Four is the number for universality. Judgment on this western world is to be held in obeisance until the sealing of the 12 tribes (vv. 2-8) and the sealing of the Gentile believers (vv. 9-10). They will be saved from death during the great tribulation (last 3½ years) (v. 14). They will dwell on earth and serve God. Compare to Revelation 21:3-4. This is the heavenly Jerusalem in the eternal state.

Note in the naming of the 12 tribes that Dan is not named. Many Bible scholars believe that the anti-Christ will be from Dan. (Gen. 49:17).

Chapter 8

The opening of the 7th seal. There is silence in heaven for the space of half an hour as the heavenly host stand in awe of the terrible judgments which are to fall on the earth. We are introduced to 7 angels (messengers) with the 7 trumpets.

1st Angel: One third part of trees (great men) were burnt up (Mark 8:24), and prosperity was taken from the earth (green grass) (Mark 6:39).

2nd Angel: The sea (Gentile nations) and ships speak of the commerce of this world. All commerce will be affected by this cataclysmic upheaval… one third.

3rd Angel: A great star falls. The word *"fall"* does not necessarily have a negative connotation here. According to Strongs it could also mean alight. Compare the following in Revelation where we see personages, stars or angels coming down from heaven (8:10; 9:1; 10:1; 12:9; 20:1). (I feel the latter verse to be the same as Luke 10:18 and will happen in the middle of the tribulation.) Who are these stars and angels? Wormwood may be an angel but he is empowered by God as is *Abaddon* (Hebrew), *Apollyon* (Greek) (9:11). His name means "Destroyer". Abaddon has the key to the bottomless pit so he could not be Satan nor either of the beasts as they are held there. In chapter 20:1 he lays hold on Satan and casts him for a thousand years into this bottomless pit. The mighty angel of ch. 10 is definitely Christ. Recall how God had power over evil spirits in the Old Testament (1 Sam. 16:14, 18:10, Judges 19:23, 1 Kings 22:22, 2 Chron. 21 to 22). These stars of chapters 8:10 and 9:1 are empowered of God. Even Satan cannot act unless God allows Him to (Job 1:12, 2:6).

4th Angel: One third part of the nations are smitten and wisdom, (the day shone not), is taken from man.

Chapter 9

5th Angel: Again we see a star fall from heaven who has the key of the bottomless pit. I have written somewhat of this in the previous paragraph. A great horde of evil is unleashed. The judgments are more moral than physical (vv. 5-6). These locusts had breastplates of iron showing there was no compassion shown (v 9). They had tails like unto scorpions which reminds us of Isaiah 9:15. The sting is often at the end or conclusion of a book or article (v. 10). The word for *Abbadon* is found in Job 26:6 and Proverbs 15:11, *"Destroyer"*.

The 6th Angel. Includes chapters 6:13 to 11:15. Verse 15 should be *"prepare for the hour"* and not *"an"* hour. It is a specific time period planned by God. These angels are sent forth to slay a third part of men. Here it is physical death as opposed to moral as in the first part of chapter 6:1-11, v. 21. In verse 21 the word *"sorceries"* PHARMAKEUS is one who uses drugs for any purpose (Acts 13:8), enchantments, sorcery. Our word "pharmacy" is derived from it (Gal. 5:20, Rev. 18:23).

Chapter 10

The angel that comes down (v. 1) is definitely Christ as the context shows. Christ often appeared as an angel in the Old Testament. This angel stands upon the earth and sea. Christ not only owns this world by creatorial power (Prov. 8:22-36; Ps. 33:6), but He also purchased it with His own blood. Satan is an usurper for he offered Christ that which was not his own but belonged to Christ (Matt. 4:8-9; 2 Peter 2:1).

Verse 3. The Lord has a mighty voice (Ps. 68:33).

Verse 6. God the Creator of heaven and earth.

Verse 7. *"The mystery of God"*.

Chapter 11

The two witnesses appear in the spirit of Moses and Elijah. They are likened to two olive trees (Zech. 4:3).

Verse 8. Jerusalem is given many names. Here it is called *"Sodom and Egypt"*.

Verse 15. The 7th and final angel sounds and God rightfully takes possession of this world.

Verse 18. The judgment of the dead. I take it to mean the unsaved dead. The end of this verse should strike fear into the hearts of these so-called "terrorists" of today.

Chapter 12

Parenthetical. The woman, the dragon and the child. The woman is Israel, the dragon is Satan and the child is Christ. If this is understood the passage is made clear. The fleeing into the wilderness speaks of the last 3½ years of the tribulation and not of this present dispensation (Zech. 13: 7b); *"I will turn my hand upon the little ones."* Also Matthew 24:16.

The casting out of Satan from heaven, I believe, will happen in the middles of the 7 weeks of Daniel and is the same as Luke 10:18. The Lord speaks as omniscient in Luke.

All the various names of Satan are given in verse 9 so as to leave no doubt as to who is specified. He is overcome by the blood of the Lamb. His ferociousness will be intensified toward man because he knows he has but a little time. Verse 6 would substantiate the claim that a portion of the Jewish remnant will be protected by God in the wilderness because the period of time given is 3½ years: a time.

Chapter 13

As we had two servants of God in ch. 11, we now have two servants of Satan in the 13th chapter. A trinity of evil.

The beast from the sea (Gentile nations: v. 1-10) is a figure of one who will arise from amongst the nations as a miraculous leader. He has all the characteristics of four great ancient nations in one man: Babylon, Persia, Greece and Rome. The deadly wound which is healed and causes all the world to wonder after is no doubt the miracle of a resuscitated Roman Empire. The beast from the sea leads these united nations. He receives his power directly from Satan and speaks blasphemy against God. He will undoubtedly be a Roman or Italian. He continues for 42 months (v. 5) which corresponds to 3½ years of chapter 12:14. He will speak against Christians and Christianity (v. 6), but he cannot touch them for they are in heaven.

Verses 11-18. The beast from the earth (should read land). *"Land"* in Scripture often refers to Palestine and Israel's right to it. This beast will possibly be a Danite as his tribe is not named in chapter 7 and the reference in Genesis 49:17 would also suggest this. See also Genesis 3:15.

The beast from the land or the antichrist will be the religious head, as the beast from the sea, the political one. He is an imitator of Christ (v. 11), *"like a lamb"*. He will receive his power from the first beast and will cause men to worship this one. Note use of words *"on the earth"* in verse 14. As typical of earth dwellers, these are those who live for this life and this world.

He causes all to receive the mark of the Beast. We are in the dark as to what this is as well as the number of man, 666. There has been too much speculation about this but during that time it will be clear.

Chapter 14

As those who follow the beast receive a mark so those who follow Christ will receive a mark. They will sing a new song which is not the same as the new song of chapter 5:9. There it is the song of the redeemed, here it is a song of thankfulness for deliverance.

The everlasting gospel preached to those who dwell on the earth is that of Psalm 19:1-6. God has ever had a witness to Himself in creation.

In verse 8 Babylon is introduced. This is the first mention of this idolatrous system in Revelation although Jezebel is no doubt figurative of it (Rev 2:20). Babylon is typical of a false worldly religion. More will be said of her later.

Verse 13. *"Blessed are the dead"*. Psalm 72:14; 116:15 refers also to this company of witnesses. This godly remnant will join their brethren of Revelation 6:9. They will be part of the first resurrection.

Verses 14-20. Christ, as a farmer reaps the grain with a sickle, he reaps the wicked in the land of Palestine (v. 20). *"The city"* refers to Jerusalem.

Chapter 15

Seven angels having the seven last plagues (v. 1). *"The song of Moses"*, (Ex. 15), *"The song of the Lamb"* (Rev. 5:9). The seven angels are given seven golden vials. The temple of God is mentioned numerous times in Revelation.

Chapter 16

The seven vials. In verse 2, the first vial is poured out upon the earth (land), Israel.

Verse 3. The second angel pours out his vial upon the sea; Gentile nations (v. 4). The third angel pours out his vial upon the waters. Water is not only a type of the word (Eph. 5:26), but also refreshment (Ps. 104:10-13). All that brings refreshment and enjoyment will be turned to blood (death).

The events described in chapter 16 will happen at the end of the tribulation period, and it is more God's judgment on the nations. Man's heart toward God will not change. Three times in the chapter we read that men blasphemed the name of God (vv. 9, 11, 21). In verse 13 the trinity of evil is named. From their mouths issue blasphemies and wickedness and urgings to men to war with God. Armageddon is not a single battle but a series of battles which is concluded by the Word riding out of heaven with the heavenly host (19:11-21). The Lord of Sabaoth (Rom. 9:29, Jam. 5:4), is this Lord of Hosts. Note verse 19, *"And the cities of the nations fell"* . New York, 9/11 will be nothing compared to this.

Chapter 17

Verses 1-17 is a description of Babylon *"the mother of harlots"* (v. 5). The physical Babylon of the Old Testament was utterly destroyed; the spiritual Babylon of Revelation will share the same fate. The king of Babylon in Isaiah 14 is typically Satan. He is called *"Lucifer"* (v. 12). See also Isaiah 13:20; Jeremiah 50:13, 26. The harlot will ride the beast for a short period of time (v. 7). But she will be utterly cast off and destroyed by the united nations (v. 17). Who is this woman called *"Babylon"* and *"the Whore"*? A woman in Scripture is often religion out of place (Zech. 5:7-8). It will be a confederacy of world religions, of apostate Christendom who are opposed to Christ and to what the Word of God teaches. It will be the final form that the world church will take but without reality; the Laodiceans of the last days. The woman is that great city which reigneth over the kings of the earth. Verse 9 tells us that the seven heads are seven mountains. What city of this world is renowned for its seven mountains? This is part of the mystery of the woman (17:7).

Chapter 18

This chapter is basically taken up with the character and final end of mystery Babylon. It's interesting to note verses 12 thru 13 for of all her wealth and possessions, the final and most important one is hidden, as it were, at the very end *"slaves, and souls of men"* (Gen. 14:21). The world will mourn the desolation of Babylon because of all the commercial wealth that will be destroyed. Verses 16-19 *"Ships in the sea"*. Verse 19 "Commerce". She shall be destroyed and found no more (v. 21).

Chapter 19

Now we come to the conclusion of all the woes (v. 1), *"After these things"*. In all that we have from chapters 6-18 it is interesting to see that as the Psalms end (Ps. 146-150), so also Revelation, which in many ways parallel the Psalms. Many of the Psalms are taken up with the same subject as Revelation, i.e. the suffering, godly remnant in the last 3½ years of the tribulation. Praise the Lord, of course, is Alleluia. How pleasant to come to this wonderful chapter after reading of all the horrors meted out to this world in the former chapters. *"The marriage supper of the Lamb"* is a wonderful subject for contemplation (v. 7). When will this take place? I believe the judgment seat of Christ (2 Corinthians 5:10) will take place immediately after the Rapture. Verse 10 is of extreme importance. What blessing we obtain when we bring Christ in to all prophecy. This verse could be transposed "The Spirit of prophecy is the testimony of Jesus".

Now a grand subject is introduced (vv.11-21). The Lord who is called *"The Word of God" (v. 13)* and has on His vesture and on His thigh a name written "King of Kings and Lord of Lords", descends with all the heavenly host to this earth to put down all wickedness and evil and to destroy those armies that have besieged His beloved city and people. There will be a great slaughter and Christ will reign victorious and set up His kingdom. He shall reign with a rod of iron for a thousand years (v. 15). The beast and false prophet will be taken and cast alive into the lake of fire (*Gahenna*).

Chapter 20

Verse 1. Is not this the same one as the star that fell from heaven in chapter 9:1? I cannot help but feel that it is. This angel could not be Satan for he lays hold of Satan and casts him bound for a thousand years into the bottomless pit (v. 2-3). As in chapter 12:9 his various names are given so as that there can be no mistaking who it is.

Verse 4. Now we see thrones and them that sat on them; Christ and the twenty four elders. The souls in the first part of this verse are those who were martyred in the first 3½ years, chapter 6:9. The second part of this verse are those martyred in the last 3½ years. They will live and reign with Christ a thousand years. There are 3 parts to the first resurrection:

1. At the Rapture, 1 Thess. 4:16-17.

2. Those who have been beheaded, 20:4.

3. At the end of the tribulation.

The 6th verse speaks of the second death. These would be those of 20:12.

Verses 7-10. Satan will be loosed at the end of the 1000 years of peace and will gather together an army, a multitude in number of those who gave feigned obedience to Christ during the millennium (Ps. 18:44, 66:3), (See margin of King James Version). They will be in the spirit of Gog and Magog—communism, man for man. Satan and his army will be put down immediately. Reading the book of Joel would be of great help in understanding this period. Satan meets his final horrible end being cast into the lake of fire, Gahenna, for eternity.

And now the Great White Throne is set up in heaven for Christ to judge those dead small and great, who are yet in their sins. They are banished to Gahenna for ever and ever. For all judgment is given into Christ's hands (Act 17:31). Death, that of the body, and hell or Hades, the place of the departed spirits are forever done with. This is called the second death. Gahenna was not made for man but for the devil and his angels. But where else could one go who despised the love of Christ and would have none of His way of salvation. *"Of how much sorer punishment, suppose ye, shall he be thought worthy, who hath trodden underfoot the Son of God, and hath counted the blood of the covenant, wherewith He was sanctified, and an unholy thing, and hath done despite unto the Spirit of grace"* (Heb. 10:29).

Chapter 21

And now John has a most glorious sight. I believe it is eight times in Revelation we read *"and I saw"*.

From v. 1-8 it is the eternal state wherein is the new heaven and new earth (2 Peter 3:12-13). This is called the day of God. There will be no nations then. All will be one universal people. We read more of the Lamb in Revelation than anywhere else in the Bible, but it is the rejected Lamb and this is what calls down the awful judgments of God. But please note that here it is not the name Jesus, nor Christ, nor the Son of Man that will dwell with man, it will be God Himself in the person of Christ (v. 3-4) (1 Corinthians 15:24-28). In the millennium righteousness shall reign but in the eternal state righteousness will dwell. From ch. 21:9 to ch. 22:5 we have the millennium. In verse 9 we see that the church is referred to as *"the bride, the Lamb's wife"* still a bride after a thousand years. Jacob's ladder will once again be set up and there will be sweet communion between heaven and earth (Hos. 2:21-22).

One will never understand prophecy unless one understands that God has two purposes, an earthly and a heavenly. There are two Jerusalems, an earthly and a heavenly, and Christ has two brides, an earthly (Song of Solomon) and a heavenly (Rev. 19:7).

I will leave the description of the Holy City to the reader's own meditation and study.

Chapter 22

The first five verses are part of ch. 21. Verse 4 *"they shall see His face"* blessed anticipation (2 Cor. 4, John 14:9). *"And His name shall be in their foreheads,"* (v. 4) perfect identification. The mitre Aaron wore proclaimed *"Holiness to the Lord"* (Ex. 28:36). But beloved His name shall ever be on our foreheads. *"It shall always be upon his forehead"* (Ex. 28:38).

And finally we have these blessed words *"Behold I come quickly"* repeated thrice. The first time (v. 7) is in connection with the keeping of His word. The second time (v. 12) is in connection with one's work, and the third (v. 20) is in connection with His return.

The final invitation *"come"* is given three times in verse 17. I pray God that every reader of these notes has answered His gracious invitation for He is soon coming for His own, *"even so, come, Lord Jesus. Amen"*.

Other Writings by the Same Author

Tracts

Samson or Life Out of Death
Compromise
Faith
Friendship
The Epistles of John
Leviticus
Proverbs
Revelation
Ruth

Books

Isaiah
Poems of a Wayfarer
Song of Solomon
Psalms and the Godly Remnant

For extra copies, please contact

MGL Multilingual
1225 E. Alexander Ave.
Tacoma, WA 98421 USA